Global Warming - Time Stories

Seeds of Sorrow

Seeds of Hope

Foreword

The Global Warming - Time Stories, **Seeds of Sorrow** and **Seeds of Hope** are about now and the coming future.

It always seems as if there are two possible Histories of Humankind, 'being unveiled' before us. For where we are and where we could be – or what we are and what we could become. These are like two different rivers that flow through 'Time'. These stories are about the haunting realities and effects of one river and the attempts to swim against the current in the other. They are short works about our two possible histories told from the future backwards, each containing three stories within one story.

Seeds of Sorrow are sad stories but with contained Hope, there is no humour, but they are not negative. There's an underlying thread connecting them, like an underground river that flows regardless of what you see above, which is in essence about the veil of sleep or darkness that seems to cover humanity, and yet there is a ray of light in that disturbing and paradoxically comforting darkness.

In Seeds of Sorrow you will read about three different people, three different times, three days of each life. Connected and affected by the effects of Global Warming and the struggle for resources and survival on a planet heating up quicker than it should be.

The stories of **Seeds of Hope** are not sad, but as the title suggests contain hope, hope for humanity, a different path awaiting us than the path were are on at present. The stories of Seeds of Hope are about awakening the 'Hero' that lies within us all, and awakens to the need to rise and raise our voice and make a choice, to help turn the heat down before that window of opportunity, that we do have, closes. That window has a one generation time latch; it's a window that never opens again.

The barriers are great, almost insurmountable, but there is a chance. We are the last generation that can help realize this chance.

People are often at their best when involved in helping others in distress, we all are, it's inherent in our nature. We have this beautiful and incipient urge to be helpful to those in need. Our inner Hero rises to the occasion. We all have one, but it's just like they say in ancient stories of old, the Hero must awaken to this call, and you never know what might awaken the sleeping Hero.

These stories and pictures have been drawn and extended from poems of our coming book on Global Warming - 'If All the world's a stage - it's on Fire' - which is also an artistic, but different attempt on bringing awareness to this theme.

Global Warming - Time Stories

Seeds of Sorrow

Seeds of Hope

General Design/Layout: Blue Light Series

Author: Martin Ray

Cover Design/Illustrator/Artist: Melanie Wichlein

Copyright: Blue Light Series 2016

Second Edition 2016

ISBN-13: 978-1523313921

ISBN-10: 1523313927

Other books in the Blue Light Series
Computer Comfort – (A modern approach to computer use)
Running Types (2016)

Global Warming - Social Story Poems
(Social commentaries on Global Warming Awareness)
If 'all the world's a stage', it's on fire. A Sense of Global Warming

Stories of Lala – Stories of Hope – Children's stories
Stories of Lala II – Creatures of the Forest (2016)

CONTENTS

Seeds of Sorrow 3

A Riddle 3

The world that was 5

Rising Seas, Falling Birds 17

Death by Drone 29

Front Cover Pictures 36

Seeds of Hope 49

A Riddle of a Rhyme of Time 49

River of a different Time 51

The Culture of Contemplation 73

Rise of the Heroes 89

Seeds of Sorrow

A Riddle

At-tension to the beginning – for that's where the end has its roots

Some words are just words, some words are more, others make rhymes, some words can be a riddle, a riddle can be how a riddle should be, and sometimes it takes a riddle to allow one to see. It depends on what you think and if you could, if so, that would be good, for a riddle is in need of someone to read.

Through the interesting concept of cause and effect, logically the causes lie in the past, for that would be the first in succession through what we call time.

But if time is only our perception of our conception of it, then perhaps our concept or our perception may be a little faulty. If time does turn into itself and it is indeed ever-last, then the cause of the effect may lie in the future, which was the past, which was the future, which was the past…and so on and so forth…you get the point…it's obviously hard to come to the end or even the beginning of an everlasting circle. Unless of course it's like those little spiral toys that kind of walk themselves down the stairs, once you give them the needed shove. In that case, circular spiralling ever repeating time may just about make sense. But, remember, riddles aren't meant to make sense, at least not at first; otherwise it wouldn't be a riddle now, would it?

The world that was

Day one

'Live well' were his father's last words as his own life energy left his body. Those words contained so much of what his father had been teaching him all his short life. The boy had survived a few years now; he was still young, barley in his 20's. He was remembering his father's words as he found the water that wasn't there. There were only memories that came in flashes, like the lightning bolts in the sky, of which there were so many now. They had increased so much since he had been a child that if he did not possess flash memories from childhood, he would think that this is always how it is and always had been, those images in the night-sky were so striking in their beauty, 'Sky-Art' his mother had called it. It never stopped. You could always see it somewhere in the distance. The boy would soak it into his being before it was time to go underground. Soon he settled to make a hidden fire, the way he was taught to do.

The memories came in flashes. He remembered the stories. The incredible Heat had started without too much fuss, the big giants of older times controlled all that, the 'mind manipulators' they were called, those that suppressed the truth, the truth of what was coming, the change, the dramatic change. They thought that they, the ones in control would survive, that they could build palaces and protect themselves.

Dad always said it was variables, too many variables, variables always sounded a little too dangerous for his liking; too many of them to control or take care of... He had to admit, he didn't really know what variables were, but they sounded pretty bad to him. When he had asked his dad if the variables would come attacking in the darkness of the night, his dad had laughed, the only time he saw him laugh since his mother died.

It was the manager's business, they miscalculated, they didn't count on the variables. They believed in their Goddess, she was called 'Propaganda', she controlled the markets. She was a powerful Goddess. All the 'Managers of Global Policy' believed in the 'markets', which were some types of laws that they said the poor did not understand, so the managers had to take care of them. At least that's what all the poor people were told, which by then was almost everybody left on the planet.

They, the 'Managers' called her by just the first two letters of her name, they were so familiar with her and she spoke to them directly, 'PR', they called her; she was their Goddess, for aeons....

The poor, who called themselves the '99', eventually pulled her statues down, tall statues that no one person could climb, it took teams of the '99' with ropes, days of climbing, securing, daring, many died, for those statues were protected. The managers had many weapons, ground weapons, flying weapons, machines of destruction that could see you, speak to you by name, and talk about how they would find the people you knew, they knew their names as well and showed pictures of them on their 'face-screens'.

He was told they knew everything. But even so, eventually they lost. The '99' took control of the palaces where the Goddess and the managers lived. Once their guards died out and their energy machines wore down, the '99' moved in on them and sacrificed them to their own Goddess, 'PR'...

At least that's what the stories said that he had heard and it sounded true. Why lie about that, there's nothing left to gain by not saying the truth. People said they knew the truth these days and the truth was the Death Heat.

Now there was only survival, to make it through the night. There were parts of the planet some said were people could still survive well, for a while, if you could get there. Some grouped up to sail the water boats that were still around. They had sails, like from ancient times, no more machines.

He saw 'hollow-bilds' once, images of how it all looked long ago, they ran on the energy of the sun, but there were not many machines left that could still do that, and no-one knew how they worked anymore. They just used them till they stopped working, but what they showed was a dream.

What lands left were hard to reach, people couldn't travel very far, you couldn't be outside in the hottest part of the day, no-one could, so all movement was time limited. You had to travel with a group, and that was tough for living, but for some there was no choice, some still called themselves the '99', but most didn't know why anymore.

Those that travelled on the open water promised to return and tell what they found, but no-one ever came back. No-one knew why, most likely dead. They had to take all the food they could carry, the sea animals weren't for eating. Some looked ok, he saw a few once, but the people who ate them died badly, the water was acid. Very little lived there now, but no one was sure, it was too dangerous even to wash in it. Some said it was the 'unclear' energy from the manager's power palaces that poisoned it slowly. All that lived nearby human and non-human changed and died. People moved away a long time ago, no-one went near those places anymore, only death filled those areas, distorted death.

All those memory thoughts flew through his mind as he stroked the fire, in this part of the world he needed a fire at night, it got cold here at night, quickly, and the fire was necessary in case the hunters came before he went underground. He couldn't risk going down to Earth too early, that was just as dangerous. There weren't many predators, but they were dangerous, it was their thirst for liquid, blood liquid, any blood. He continued making his throw fire-arrows, he made them almost without thinking, but always while sensing, that kept him aware anyway.

Only bands of men or the blood hunters could come in the darkness of night and the throw arrows were his only real defence in the darkness. Once he'd been attacked by a gang of six with howling dogs, at the end there was only him and nine burning fires. No one expects the fire arrows in this climate, his dad told him that.

He sung a quiet song, in the way he was taught to remember by his mum.

We don't believe your Goddess, she told us all lies,
for as death was all around, she had shiny sparkly eyes.
A smile always she wore upon her face.
The 'mind managers' were the ones that killed the human race.
We don't believe in your Goddess any more
as the acid seas rise upon our shore.

The 'mind managers' destroyed the books,
to stop the '99' from seeing how it all really looks.
Way back in the past where our future was cast
like dice in a game, nothing was the same.

They stopped people learning how to read,
said it was something we'd never need.
Music also was a thing of the past; you couldn't hear it anymore,
now the dice was cast.
The people discovered it was all lies
what they were told with sparkling eyes,
too late to change it now
but we must remember somehow.

The boy had found a book once or at least he thought it could have been a book. The managers were said to have destroyed them all, so they could control what people remembered, then they wouldn't get the blame for the 'net' they had cast over the world. It must have been a big 'net'; it caught everything and anyone, almost.

There were some that didn't believe in the Goddess called 'PR', those people hid some books, paper made from trees. How they did that, the boy had no idea, what he found once could have been a book, but it dusted and disappeared so quickly when he took it out of its protector. If it was a book its protector must have had a leak. It wouldn't have mattered he couldn't read anyway, only a few could still do that.

Some of the older ones said that the managers lived in cities, he'd seen a 'hollow-bild' of a city but those 'hollow-bilds' were from before the seas covered much of the lands. His dad said many big cities were on the coast, so those were the first to go, then the countries got smaller.

As the boy pushed the embers of the fire around, the 'Sky-Art' danced in the distance, it continued for hours, but it wasn't coming in his direction, no, his direction was turning into desert, little rain came here. Yet in other places it never stopped. It was the beauty of the 'Sky-Art' night, unless you were unlucky and trapped in the force of the storm, but generally he kept a good distance.

Some of the older ones had seen the abandoned cities underground; the managers had built them to hide from the heat. It was cooler down there, but then it all changed again, the storms took care of all that and water or sand now covered those cave cities.

His dad said that some of those 'managers' had built mountain cities, they covered their old towns with glass and built deeper in the ground as well, so they lived in the mountain.

They survived for a long time, maybe some even till now. No-one knows for sure. But eventually many ran out of food, and the food they grew in the mountains, in the dark, made them ill in their bodies and they had no more little ones to continue.

His dad said that probably only the 'Travellers' and the bands of Robbers he called the 'Men-Beasts' now survived. The 'Travellers' were those who continued the old ways, who could find the water that seemed not to be there. They moved from area to area, sleeping and resting in the coolness of the Earth and rising to travel in the cooler part of the day. The 'Travellers' and the 'Men-Beasts' had their own different ways of survival.

His dad said the sea water had risen a lot and covered much land, and that the planet would probably cool itself eventually, but it would take time, a long time for us. There will be no people left then. It will Heat more before it cools down again.

Dad said the planet lived, breathed and slept and waked, that each dawning day was the same as our out-breath, and each lightening dark night was its in-breath. But he also said the same about the tides of the Ocean, so he wasn't sure anymore what to think, but as we counted time, the planet counted it slower, which meant, it would take a few days of its own time to recover itself; but for us that would be many thousands of years, and we'd all be long gone by then. The earth would recover and continue. He said the 'Travellers Stories' told that, and there was no reason to not believe them.

For a while a dark deadness had covered some of the earth, followers of the 'Goddess PR' fought amongst themselves. The bigger ones destroyed the smaller with such violence it had spared almost none; they called it the 'Drone Death'.

At first they said they were there to help to control the water rising, and to help keep order as the waters took over the lands a little bit every day. People moved 'en masse', but then, 'they' started to kill them...

The boy sung another story to remember, his mum said he had to remember. The managers had made people forget. Some of us had to remember.

The fish in the sea all died, the people watched them float and cried.
Acid burned their bodies raw, but only the fishermen really saw.
No longer could the people eat the fish that once tasted sweet.
Life had changed; it was no longer a treat.

Land animals died a thirsting or starving death,
for nothing grew for them to eat,
to eat another was their only way,
some survived, just some they say.

And now they hunt us in the dark of night,
for it's too hot in days light.
The rising tides covered lands,
but the heat also brought more sands.

Of dunes there were many now,
no seeds would grow anyhow.
Some roots people had learned to eat and survive
but life that was, no longer thrived.

They took the blood from the earth,
and burned it up till it was a darkly death.
It made them move around so fast,
even in the sky, but it didn't last.

They called it oil and it was plenty,
it greased the planet as it was 'meanti'.
As they took it out, the planet slowly bled,
it heated all and left us dead.

It took a while for them to find
that the planet had its own mind,
it had a body and a soul
and in its emotions we left a hole.

A little planet, the child of a young sun,
and like a mother it cared for its young,
it brought the balance once again and got rid of the virus,
that was them - us.

All this time he had been digging, the way he was taught to by his father. He dug deep, prepared his airbag and air-stick and sleep came to him.

Day two

From the moment the rays hit the ground it was boiling Hot beyond belief, the hottest day ever felt on human skin. The boy was deeper than normal but even that was only just bearable, he could feel it was going to be a 'Hot one'. The Heat penetrated through his 'air-stick'. He stayed much longer under earth but at least he knew nothing would come to the attack, in this Heat nothing could move, you'd dry and fry. The skin would burn, everything that still lived hid in the dark until the late afternoon shadows came, and then it was only a bit milder.

As the sun was setting each day, the shadows were cast over the drying landscape, the mixture of the blue sky and the dark clouds played beautiful tricks with the eyes, enchanting if you kept aware, deadly if you didn't, every shadow could be danger. His dad had shown him how to build the layer and repair the airbag when necessary; his dad said if he looked after it, it would last the whole life. Almost every night he had to make a new layer, if he was on the move and usually he was. It was the only way to survive.

The hottest of the day had passed; time to move before the blood hunters came, their power smell was better than dogs. The managers had made them; the boy didn't know how they did that, what strange powers they had way back then. Some had escaped their handlers and now hunted and killed anything that moved.

He moved slowly upwards out of the earth, it was Hot, this day had been hotter than ever, and he didn't know how long that had been that way. You couldn't tell years any more, time seemed always the same more or less. He had some hours left before he'd have to dig again. He could stay there but there's no way of telling if his smell was carried in the direction of the blood hunters. He moved, hiding his tracks sometimes as he went, just as he was taught to do.

After a while he heard shouting, wild shouts, from those who did not care to be quiet, and use sound to induce fear. They were usually robbers, no-one hunted them except blood hunters, but the blood hunters rarely attacked large bands of men for they always had weapons of danger. The shouts were like orders, they were hunting something or someone, but that usually meant both, if the robbers didn't need to slave you, they cooked you. But that meant their place was nearby, they couldn't travel far in Heat, no-one could.

In a short while from a hiding place he could see them; he knew he was invisible to them, that he was sure about.

He could see who they were hunting, a girl, she moved like him, almost unseen, but she was in panic because the robbers had dogs, just for that purpose, to hunt and find meat. There were eight in all, five men and three women, he knew they'd find her soon; so did they and she too.

He remembered his mother's words, she sung them so many times, he surrendered to the memory of it as he moved swiftly... His body moved with its own speed, his mind at a different speed, he sung the words softly.

> There will be times of special needs
> and we are the last of a sacred breed,
> we can help and we must do what we can,
> to save the child of woman and man.

> When we see a Being in need,
> help and care is our creed.
> In man there is an Angel and a Beast,
> in times of difficulty the beast will be released.
> The Angel can do nothing until he has been called,
> and so few know how to call today,
> it was an old and sacred way.

> We must do all we can
> to save people from the beast in man.

> As man turns into the beast,
> upon human flesh he will feast,
> these days are upon us now,
> we must avoid it somehow.

The boy moved across the land, he made the calling sound that only the girl would know. He saw her slow down to listen, her body expanded in awareness, he sounded the direction for her to go, she came, the robbers knew nothing, but the dogs caught a sent, they ran ahead of the group.

The boy appeared in front of the girl, her heart lightened; the boy moved swiftly, he took the dogs out with fire arrows, a dangerous thing to do in this Heat. The fires danced together, a raging Heat spread everywhere, the deadwood and dried out grass burned at an incredible pace. No-one made fire in the Heat.

He grabbed the girl and moved with silent speed, even though they had no more need of silence, they ran... needing no camouflage, no dogs could follow, the robbers were as good as blind; the fire followed them, if they could not escape, they die today.

When they were safe and rested they replenished their water that wasn't there from the deep, they both could find it easily enough, they just had to dig to find the insects first. Then they buried down, necessary, for the night was coming.

As they were two, they dug deep and quick, the boy always had two digging tools as a safety. They spent the first part of time replenishing the fire arrows; they made many, and fire arrows were always their deadly speciality. As they burned they could never be copied, their secrets burned with them. The girl was of a similar tribe, unknown to him. But they shared the same ancient stories and both were happy just 'to be'.

In the night they shared the songs of their mothers they were almost the same, another real way to give recognition as to how close they really were. They knew there were not many of them left; they made union together, in case it was still possible to continue the tribe, and because they had normal desires of cares and needs.

Day three... Became the Hottest day known to Humankind; there was no day for them. They died in each other's arms.

A long time before

Rising Seas - Falling Birds

Day One

Her training over the years increased, just like the Heat. She was taught to dig every night now, and prepare the airbag that they would need under-earth, all her tribe were. The outsiders were never to know, it was too dangerous to show them our ways, with the digging tool, dig deep and fast, cover the tracks, leave no signs, always making air filters and arrows, that and how to find water in the deep ground, where there was none to be found, to look for the special insects that show there was hidden nourishment deep down there. At the moment they were still collecting the waters of the morning dew, but that would change.

Everyone was taught the stories to remember, it was the only history possible anymore. Her mother had sung the stories long into the night, almost every night while they watched the 'Sky-Art'. It was the only way they could remember now, everything else had been taken.

She'd seen a book, but her father said it didn't mean anything anymore and it would dust when the protector broke down.

She loved the morning mist, it sparkled, it only lasted a short time before the day started to heat, it had always been this warm, she didn't know it ever to be cooler, but she believed the history songs of the older ones.

At the moment they all lived together, they didn't need to dig deep to survive yet, but they said that time was upon us. We had prepared for this a long time now.

The time is now here when we divide into small groups. The spreading time had started, anxiety was all around, some say we should have all spread already, but no-one wanted to leave.

It was dangerous to stay together longer; large tribes of robbers would attack in the 'early-eve'. It had happened in the last place they lived. The elders used fire arrows to defend; it burned everything, even their home. The girl sung to herself quietly to remember:

> Our home is never in one place for long,
> we must travel and wherever we are, we belong.
> We can never stay long enough for them to see
> that we do things differently.
> Man is the beast now, and we must survive them somehow.
> We cannot survive any longer as a band,
> now we must travel and spread over the land
> our planet is becoming slowly dead.

She didn't want to leave her tribe, but people had been leaving for days now, heading in every direction. She was frightened but she would be with a few others still.

In the early-eve the history stories were told, her father was a story teller, so he began to speak first.

The PR Drone-War began casually enough, at first it was just a new weapon, but then the Global Managers made it the weapon of choice for all, cheap, deadly, all seeing, silent death, except for the buzzing sound, but even that disappeared with the new ones. And for the victims, no-one to fight back against, no enemy stands before you ready to die, a life for a life.

When the masses started to work out what was happening, they protested, the Drones turned on them, population control became population kill. The mass migrations ended in death, no-one wanted all the extra people coming into their lands so they killed them at their borders. Every country by then had Drones, so every country killed.

No one could count how many died. Confirm, deny, confirm, deny, went through the airwaves, but they too were now under control mostly, only some stories escaped and went public for a while, before being removed from history. No-one knew the truth anymore. A digitally monitored and controlled history re-written as it happened. Whenever any information got through the Global Net - for a while - people said it 'Snowed' today or there's some 'Snow' about. Just like snow used to come, you would see it and then it would disappear.

Someone once called it the "Memory - Hole", this was a very deep Hole indeed. As the years passed millions fell through that hole and died.

The rich went to their underground cities for a while, but sometime later even they ran out of food. By that time the memory of it all was different, probably due to that Hole being so deep.

At some point they ran out of oil and many natural resources, no people wanted to work that anymore and none could, too Hot to be outdoors in the Heat of the day, for a while they went solar and wind, but only for a while.

Rising acid seas - food chain dying out - natural life withering in the scorching sun, it was as if we had pulled the sun closer towards us and it stayed.

After a short silence for reflection he continued.

Deception and Distraction – Destruction and Death

At first people thought it was something called Imperialism, that's where one country tries to dominate other countries than their own. As that had been happening for most of History it wasn't anything new. We didn't know why of course, our little rocky barren country had nothing anyone would want. They didn't need slaves anymore, they had enough of them, called 'economic slaves', from deals with other countries for cheap labour and their own poor, they were not excluded.

They couldn't keep their own underprivileged too poor of course, otherwise they wouldn't have enough money to buy what was being produced, business was global and the corporations wanted the world.

But there was oil and what's called natural resources, gas, trees, minerals, our country had plenty of minerals. So they probably wanted them anyway, but so many other countries had them as well, it just didn't make sense to kill or control everybody for minerals, no, people discovered much later what really happened, too late to do anything about it.

The 'Managers' knew the world was Heating and they knew the problems that would come with that, Global Warming meant wars of resources, water mostly, but food and liveable land as well.

It was never said openly but it was in the planning, control as much as possible, they knew it would take possibly decades to get slow access to everywhere, but that was what they were after, through sub-diffuse; deception and Distraction leading to Destruction and Death. Country after country fell under the Great Beast of purpose called 'Interests of Empire'.

As time passed the climate became too dramatic for it to be 'media managed' anymore, no longer could they claim 'strange weather patterns', 'abnormalities', Dramatic Change became the normal.

Populations of different countries tried to protest but it was too late. The 'Goddess' called 'PR' had subdued the '99' too long, they had no power left, despite what they were led to believe about the society they lived in. The corporations not only controlled the governments they were the governments.

They were the rich and they were protected. But only from the masses, not from the effects of the climate, at least not for long, events cascaded out of control after a short time, but we jump ahead of our history, my dear family.

But how did they get to be so bad?

We don't know, but we think it happened over time, with their 'media manipulation' combined with the desire to make money; they manipulated their young away from the necessities of life, and installed the urge to be selfish and uncaring about beings in general.

Over decades their 'entertainments' became more violent, they thought it was better to have more realistic entertainment, their young liked it more. Of course this is true - but at a price - that cause had an effect, no longer able to feel the false reality of the situation the characters on a screen were in, their fantasy world took control.

Death became meaningless, with no consequences, a game! Gradually their violence increased at home, they spread it over the world. They kept their population poor so the young had to join the military, which in their fantasy and controlled minds was patriotic for their needy countries. The managers used all situations that they could to manipulate and guide to their 'disastrous' benefit.

But that is not the whole story; these unfortunate 'children of empire' paid their own price as well. Those who controlled the manipulating war machine conditioned out of their children the 'sacred and inborn' feelings of 'empathy' for others. They suffered in their minds and souls or in their words 'went crazy'. Returning from war and killing their own family members or other children of empires, killing for killing's sake, but sooner or later they killed themselves.

One final detail of this sad answer to your question daughter is that men, who mostly are the ones who go to war, don't become men until they are in their fortieth year of existence, more or less. Before that time, they are still boys, emotionally, no matter what they do in life, there are exceptions, but this is the rule. It's boys that go to war and kill, if they survive, that means they are men that have killed when still young boys. That does not fare well for any nation that wants to be healthy. Unfortunately this sadness has mostly always been so.

It's rare that the leader or manager of an empire has ever blooded his soul or hands with the direct killing of others, if so, they might think twice about sending boys off to kill and be killed in their body and in their soul. For the rest of the evening, others told the History stories. She lay beside her mother while they watched the 'Sky-Art', in the distance, beautiful, deadly and changing. Above their own heads were the never changing glistening stars, so compact, she was sad she couldn't see them in the day, the blue veil of the sky dropped over earth, and it was Hot. The 'un-veiling' of the Universe only came at sundown. Her mother's words reminded her.

The 'Sky-Art' there is now to see,
that nature changes how all will be.
The Heat destroys everything now,
in order for it to begin again somehow.
It must bring a balance back from this un-human attack
that was unleashed by the beast in man.
We cannot tell how the world will be,
we can only feel, sense, watch and see.

Day Two

As she was making preparation for the coming day, her mother's voice spoke in her mind.

Sense the moment now, live somehow,
all beings alive have that aim,
we must hold the level of humanity,
but we must try to be different in the main,
because we are more than we can see.
Humans were special but they lost their way,
they go the way of all alive, it's happening day by day,
the sun burns everything, nothing will survive.

Our tribe is of an ancient time,
we have always had our ways,
we go back before man recorded time
and we have survived till the end of days.
The teaching has always been oral,
told from one to another prepared,
never was it placed in books,
and only with the 'ready' was it ever shared,
and remember, nothing is ever how it looks.

The words, as they always did, caused her to 'collect' herself together, she realized, like some of the others, she was scattered, in thought and body, living in fear of the future, when she had been taught to live in the moment, full sensing, feeling, and watching, and simply remember the past.

Not to be lost in the past, not to be trapped by it, nor to regret and lose the beauty of the present moment, but to remember and learn. She held the moment, everything around her highlighted, she could see her thoughts come; she let them pass like birds, holding onto none. That was from the old teaching, when there were birds. She was sensing the hot air, silently being.

And that's what she must pass on to her child, if she had the chance.

The day passed in preparations and silent goodbyes, knowing that everyone they see would be for the last time. Most will never meet again.

Only small groups could now 'Travel' and survive together. Life: as we know it will now change. The Heat increase will soon force us underground for much of the 'Hot' part of the day, with that change, different dangers will now come.

If she ever has a child, life will now be different from what she has known, to live in 'common - protection' with others is no longer possible. It was a day of sadness and recognition of reality.

She must part from her parents and travel with others, for the same blood cannot mix, so the families all separate. There was a heavy sadness she had never seen before in her parents' eyes. They had lived this way all their life, so the change for them would be dramatic. She and her sister were still young and had been prepared, this had always been the coming future and it was now.

For her it was like the next step into adulthood, dealing with life, relating to necessity. The dangers were real. The heat, after the Heat came finding enough nourishment, it was still possible, that they had been taught. No, the other dangers were more of a threat. The beasts of prey, there weren't many of them, but the other was 'Man' or as her mother called them, the 'Man-Beast'. The savagery of these people had increased over the years. Goodness had left them, and if there was no 'Goodness' there was only evil.

Her mother said it wasn't their fault, that was the way things had to go. It happened when people had no civilising moral centre; it led the way back to barbarism. That path had begun long ago. It began when they were poisoning the air and started to 'speed heat' our planet.

There were civilizing movements but they were weak and not enough, the pendulum started to swing when they were still building their great cities. A civilization dying through growth greed, there were no leaders with conscience. The system they lived under blocked all possibility of change.

They worshipped the Goddess of Greed,
they had no leaders with 'Being' enough to lead.

The death of culture came quick, just like the Heat, all systems were interconnected on the planet, the chain reaction began. But time plays strange tricks; day by day it never seemed so bad. Causes were explained away; even the many wars that existed were explained away, people could see no relation between all the different effects, not realizing their world changed before their eyes.

Tomorrow they would leave, all the preparations are done. She sung to her little sister the song of Hope: **H**aving **O**nly **P**ositive **E**motions.

There is always a song of hope,
it's written in your heart,
you will hear it in difficult times,
it will help you cope;
always remember what's real and fine.

Sense while you look - feel while you think.
From the normal food of life all people drink,
but this is special in its way, for it's a song of hope every day.

It's a silent song to sense and feel,
it separates you from what's unreal.
It will strengthen you every day.
When you have fear in any way,
your fear will not be real,
it's just you forget the song of hope,
you must stay in the present moment to cope,
then fear itself will disappear,
for the silent inner song always brings Hope near.

As her sister slept, for a while she lost her own 'Song of Hope' and recounted in sadness.

A bird fell from the sky, it didn't know why.
The first of many that did fall,
and then it rained from heaven, birds all.

On the ground they were eaten by the beast of prey,
little did they know that no pleasure came their way.

After a while they too passed away…
and so the story goes,
'One man's meat is another man's poison'.

She missed the singing of the morning birds, for there were none left to sing or to take the seeds of life and drop them where they will, they travelled no more. It was too Hot to fly, only die.

No water to wet their little parched lips,
their life giving energy slipped away from their wingtips.
What birds were left no longer sung, only cried
then died their silent death, they dropped like stone.

Hardly anyone slept long that night knowing they must part tomorrow. The sadness of the spreading, but it was the only way for them to survive now, some might make it to continue into the next generation of what time was left.

Day three

The morning mist was everywhere, thick like never before, but of course it was like that every day now at this time. Only the Dark Death Birds flew in the silver piercing greyness of the morning bursting sun. Shadows all, graceful, there was still magic to be seen, but they were Death itself. She could feel it in her heartbeat, her always present heartbeat, but one day soon even that would stop. If her heart could cry it would flood up with tears for her inner thoughts became her fears.

She was cold, some thoughts she couldn't hold, for they chilled her heart to
the bone and left her all alone. She knew why?
She was told she had to remember to transmit from the past, for time here
wouldn't last; her time now would become times past.

She remembered the words she was told,
the words her father said must be bold.
Her tribe must remember what took place,
and the words must be remembered, like a face.
There is no other way to remember and keep a track
for the 'Beast in Man' is always on attack.

In the past, long ago now, even before her father's father was born,
many of her tribe died the 'Cutting Death',
small bits of metal travelled through your body
slicing anything on their way;
the organs did not survive more than a day,
the 'cutting edge' of their technology.

They experimented with their bombs and the children born
became 'the nation of the deformed',
they didn't live very long.
Their doctors came and looked what their bombs had blooded.
They were perfecting their ways of inhuman conduct,
something they studied.

The morning was spent with everyone being in a sad soft awareness moment, one where they knew they would never meet again. Some will not survive for much longer, only a few will carry on the blood line and teaching of the tribe. In general, humanity has sunk to the lowest levels of barbarism and cruelty. Humans as a race die out. The increasing heat will kill off the last. This river of time has run dry.

They had the gathering like in older times, no words were said, they sat in circle, so all could see, and together they tried to be. Aware of all, that had been, that is now, and what they must do. The parting and spreading must be finished. Now Time begins anew, some may meet in future times, but their descendants will carry the rhymes of ancient past until these days, there will be some connection of these most ancient ways. For that, at least there is some hope.

A long time before – now – Present Time

Death by Drone

Day one

The buzzing sound was there again, almost every day one of them flew by, you couldn't see them, only hear them and she was told they could see you, even your face when they kill you.

They wanted us dead, but she didn't know why, why all her family had to die. She had done nothing wrong, what type of people wants to kill others that they've never even met. She was told the drones had no pilots, only cameras, the drivers of the 'Drones' sat somewhere in front of a computer, she had heard of them, but never seen one. Her father said it's like a mobile phone, only bigger, she had seen one of them; you could talk to people anywhere in the world with them, if you had the money. If she ever had one then she'd call and ask why? One day perhaps, unless they decide they don't like her dark skinned face.

But her father said even phones were dangerous to have these days. These people could see where your phone is and bomb you. It had happened to many others now, and they knew of no reason why. Once in her village a family was bombed, all dead, the whole family. She used to play with the girl, but no more. In villages nearby, this had also happened. She remembered her Fathers poem.

> When you see through the eye of a Drone,
> you don't know who it is you kill or leave all alone,
> wounded or in shock; humanity takes a walk.
> Sadly, young people are conditioned to be that way.
> Those in power play on a weakness called suggestibility.
> The young are not to blame. It's the society that's at shame.

Her father said it's something we must live with, many people wanted to control our lands, which meant trying to control the people, but he said that would never be. They can kill us, but they can't control us, they don't know our ways. He said they will kill many more of us, but eventually the invaders would leave, unfortunately leaving behind only destruction, devastation, and death. You can kill a people but you can't kill their soul, their heart, only God has that power.

She sang a song: Oh please great bird high in the sky,
don't send your fire down on us, pass on bye,
we've done nothing wrong to you,
but there's nothing we can do,
if you, with your all seeing eye, decide we should die,
that would be tragic for us,
please pass on bye. We don't want to die.

In the afternoon the women of the village finished off the making of a carpet for the wedding gift to her sister. It was filled with exotic animals that she had never seen, and the most wonderful complex designs and symbols, so rich in detail, her grandmother said, it would last for over 100 years. The girl, being young, had spent the last couple of weeks sharing her duties with another girl, standing in the centre of the circle and holding the design up for all to see.

The mothers and daughters sung often as they worked, sometimes they sang for fun, everyone happy to be working together, taking pleasure in the common sharing of their work.

Other times they began quietly, the girl was always aware that this was one of the special times, everyone would always be still; they'd sit quietly before their work. In the beginning the girl thought everybody was lost in a dream, or forgot themselves, but no, she came to realise that all the women sitting there, were aware of everything and of each other.

The song always sounded solemn and sacred at the same time, sometimes one man or another would come and play an instrument.

The women waited till the beginning of the music before singing. They never sat in the same place, nor did the same work, nor had the same neighbours, the songs, their roles, their voices all changed.

Her grandmother said that making a 'Special' Carpet was like life, always changing, but with a plan. The makers must learn to adapt to all the changing requirements, to know and understand all aspects of the craft. When the girl asked about the sacred songs, the grandmother said that's our ancient way of thanking God, and of remembering where we came from, why we're here, and what we want, and of living well. When the girl said to her Grandmother that she didn't think bombs from the sky meant we were living well, the old lady was adamant, smiled and said, we live well my child; it's those who wish to kill us who don't live well.

Later she heard her father talk about not 'living well', and that it led to our Planet Heating. The changes in our weather were so dramatic, many died and many more will. Humans in the blood thirst for oil changed the Quality of the 'sacred air', causing the planet to adapt; eventually we will be cast aside as a danger to the planet, a race of beings given so much to know, but failing to understand.

Our human race was given the possibility to lead and to look after Earth and all it contained, but had no 'Leaders of Being', no 'Leaders of Seeing', a sorry sad state of affairs. A spiritual death of societies induced and contained by 'Being-less' power seekers in control, for whom uncaring greed seems to be their only creed. It caused Humanity to lose the balance that it had been struggling to maintain ever since its existence.

This modern world, so fast, it seems it can't be stopped,
so sadly now, 'Humans' will be dropped,
unemployed as a race, no more we'll see the human face,
perhaps a few generations left to change,
but that may be just romance - that sounds strange.

Day two

Her sister was getting married tomorrow, there was hope and expectation, but the excitement was everywhere, both families would come together in celebration. It was their ancient tribal custom, so many of the old ways that her family tried to continue, in this, what her father called the modern world, full of nothing with real meaning.

We would dance the old dances; sing the old songs, to let God know we were here and celebrating. In older times they brought fireworks from over the hills from the Asian tribes, and before that my father said we lit fires, big celebration fires. Presents were given, some for hope, some for comfort, some for wealth. Times had changed, and so many invaders had tried to occupy our country, our ways were being destroyed like our land and our people. Some resisted the invaders, some tried to continue the old ways, passed down from one generation to the next, to live in peace.

Tomorrow when both families come together they would sit in circle, the sacred circle. Where there was a circle, God was present, and the young couple would be representing the 'now' - the hope for the continuation of the future, with all the past surrounding them, wishing them well. An animal would be sacrificed for celebration, but it was practical, animals weren't wasted in this part of the world, it would feed both families for the marriage ceremony, it would be a gift from her father, that and much other food that people would bring.

She was filled and brimming with excitement. A wedding, but not only, her sister's, her sister was quite contained, but she could tell, she knew her sister, her sister was more excited than she, which must be difficult.

Getting married was the continuation and union of the tribes, then children would come to continue the bloodline, human life, it was a very important day, many children her own age and younger would be there, even the oldest who could travel would come, it was much more than a union of two people, her father said it was a custom that sealed friendship and families together.

For the girl the day was spent in lost excitement going around the village talking to everybody she saw. At some point in the day everyone had come to see the carpet. Its beauty was always silently acknowledged. The girl had never seen a more wonderful work of art, except when the sun was rising or going down, or at night when the veil of the universe was lifted for all to see.

Her father said it was to remind them of how small they were. Her grandmother had said something similar but different, that the veil was lifted as the quiet time of the day came, to remind people of a sense of scale, which in the busy day we forget. For when it was evening time and the sparking sky-art of the night stars glittered, it's as if God, only in quietude, allowed the beauty and magnificent vastness of himself to be seen. Because for us the stars never moved, their time was beyond our time.

Her father sometimes used to sit through the night on the mountain and look at the stars, but no more, the weather had changed now, it was often very cold. Some days were burning hot and there was little water to drink, but the nights were cold, bitter cold. Everyone she heard speak about the weather agreed the world was warming; the seasons no longer would be the same as the years passed.

She remembered her father saying that between the constant worry of war and the lack of food and water, they will have to move. They didn't want to leave their tribe, their way of life, but it will become the only way to survive.

That night she could hardly sleep. Her Mother quietly sang an old story to help sleep come along.

> In the beginning they say all was good,
> and we were given all God could,
> sent to Earth from the stars above,
> you could see your star, if you had love.

> Times of celebration and of joy,
> soon comes times of a baby girl or boy,
> to continue our human race,
> a new child, a God with a human face.

Some cultures say new born babies are Gods
brought up within a culture
so that slowly human they become.

The union of a girl and boy to become a couple and live in joy,
and though hardship may come to all in every land,
a couple grow into a Woman and a Man.
Two halves of a human face,
joined together, it's a union and a continuation,
of our Human Race.

A child born of the human need,
another God to be born in a human seed,
for it to flower and to be, for God is and always will be.
He just spreads himself, better to see.

Day three

First missile

Red hot blood flew like magic pellets
through the hot burning and sizzling air.
They landed on her face like sticky rain and spread through her hair.
She didn't care.
The shock of her family flying by in bits; a leg, an arm, a head,
a fingertip, as they flew by her heart cried.
She shed no tear, frozen in shock with fear. The world just died.
Fallen to her knees, her heart begged quick release.
But no thoughts flew through her head,
her weeping heart silently cried.

Second missile

The red hot sticky blood ran down her dazed head, it was her sisters who just wed, blown apart; she lost her head, along with all her family.

It was a 'Drone Attack' from the sky: they couldn't see it coming, nor could they defend. A Missile from Hell was fired and brought them to their end.

She was young and did not hear the sound, for the wedding party was all around. They had stopped where now only bits of bodies will be found.

Their bodies blown apart, this is the 'Drone Art', she didn't know that this was life; just that it was no more.

The girl was all alone and dying slowly, no one left alive, just the pieces of those who had once been, her family... everywhere, but together. She closed her eyes in pain unable to see ever again.

She had to go, she couldn't wait, death was coming and he was never late. And it was always a he... The 'last impression' that flew by, cut quick and deep she couldn't scream or even sigh, her vocal cords were cut, she had no eyes left to see. Let alone to cry...Her short life passed through her head, so much to live for, just to be dead.

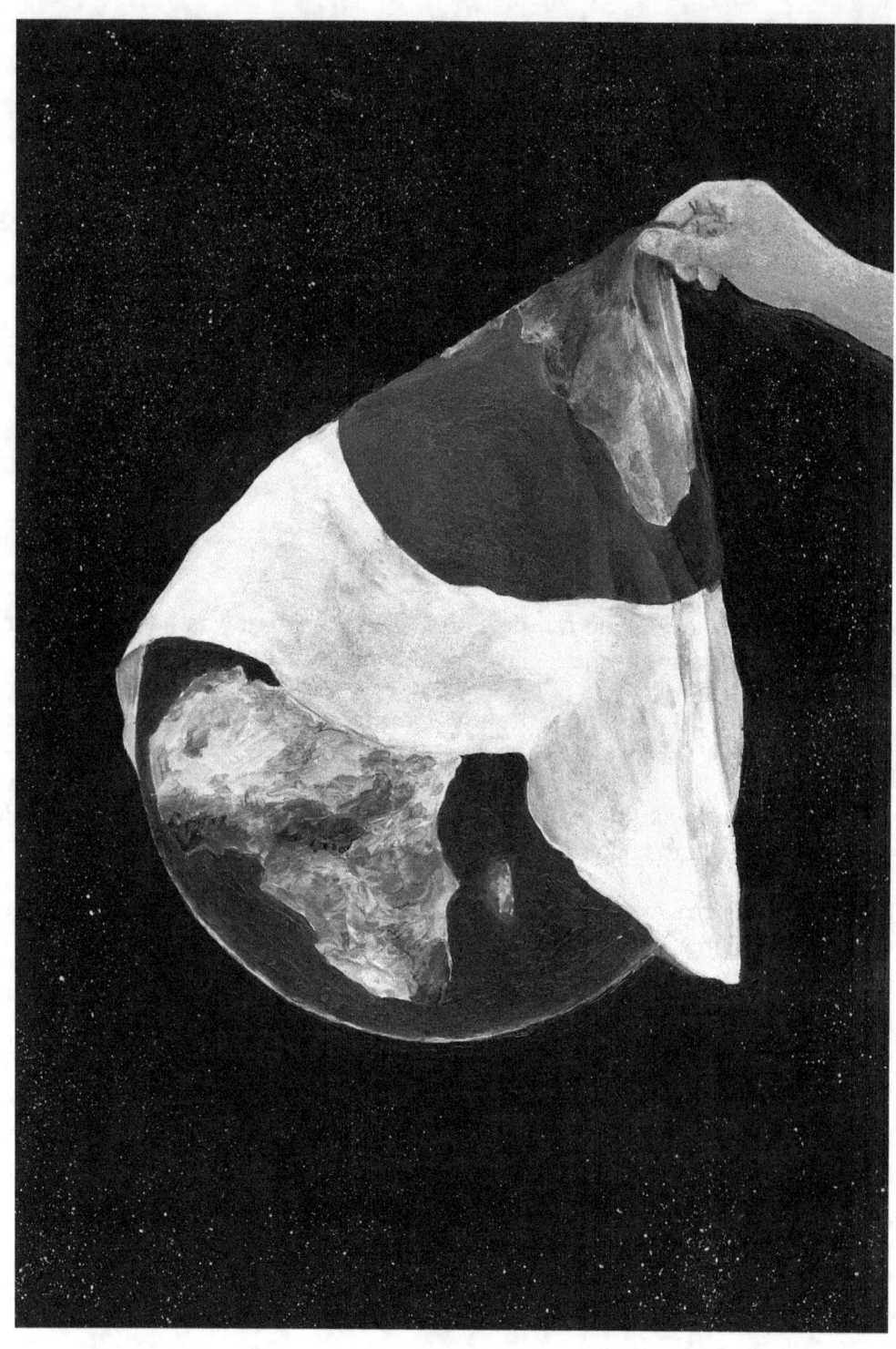

Being Unveiled

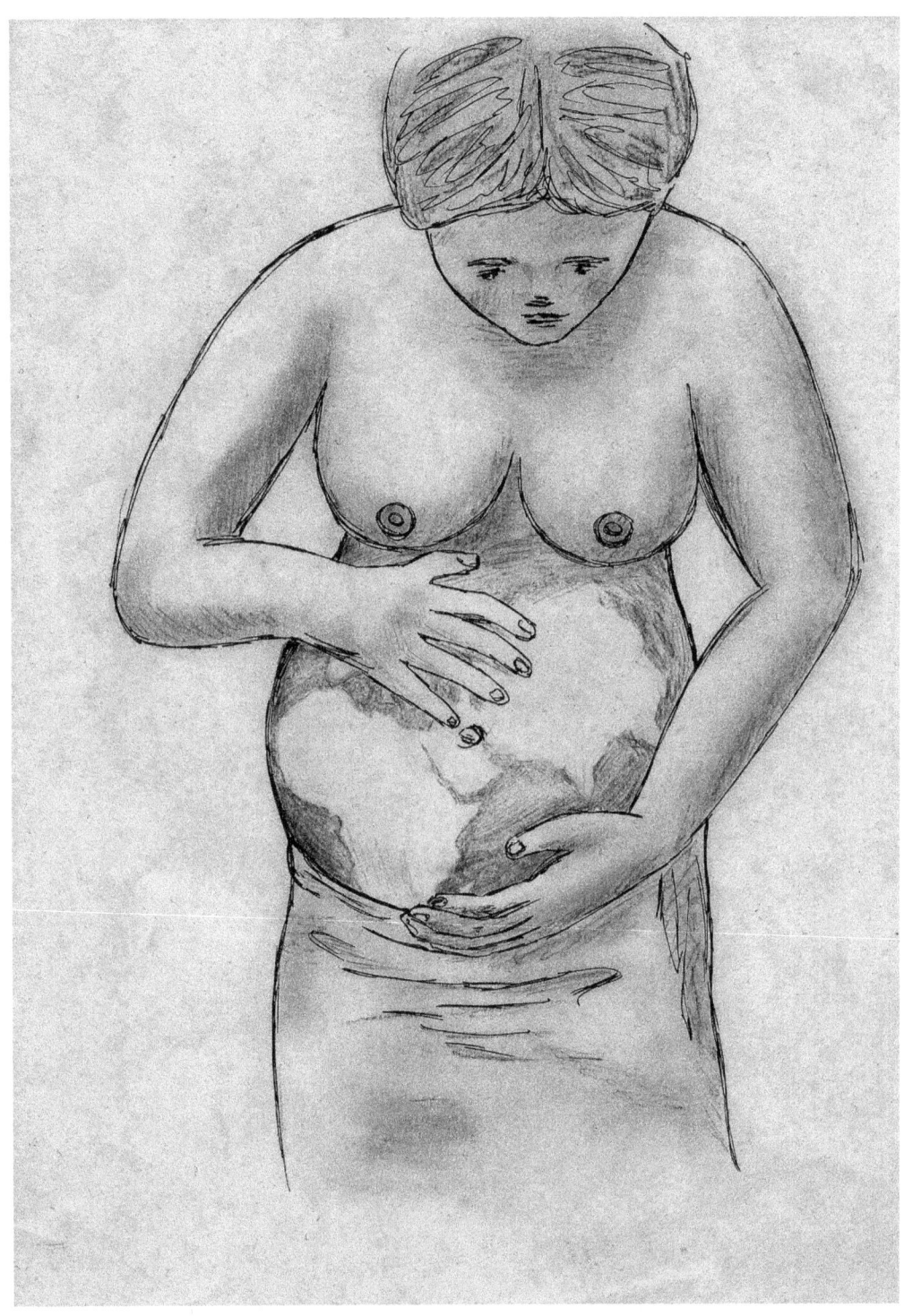

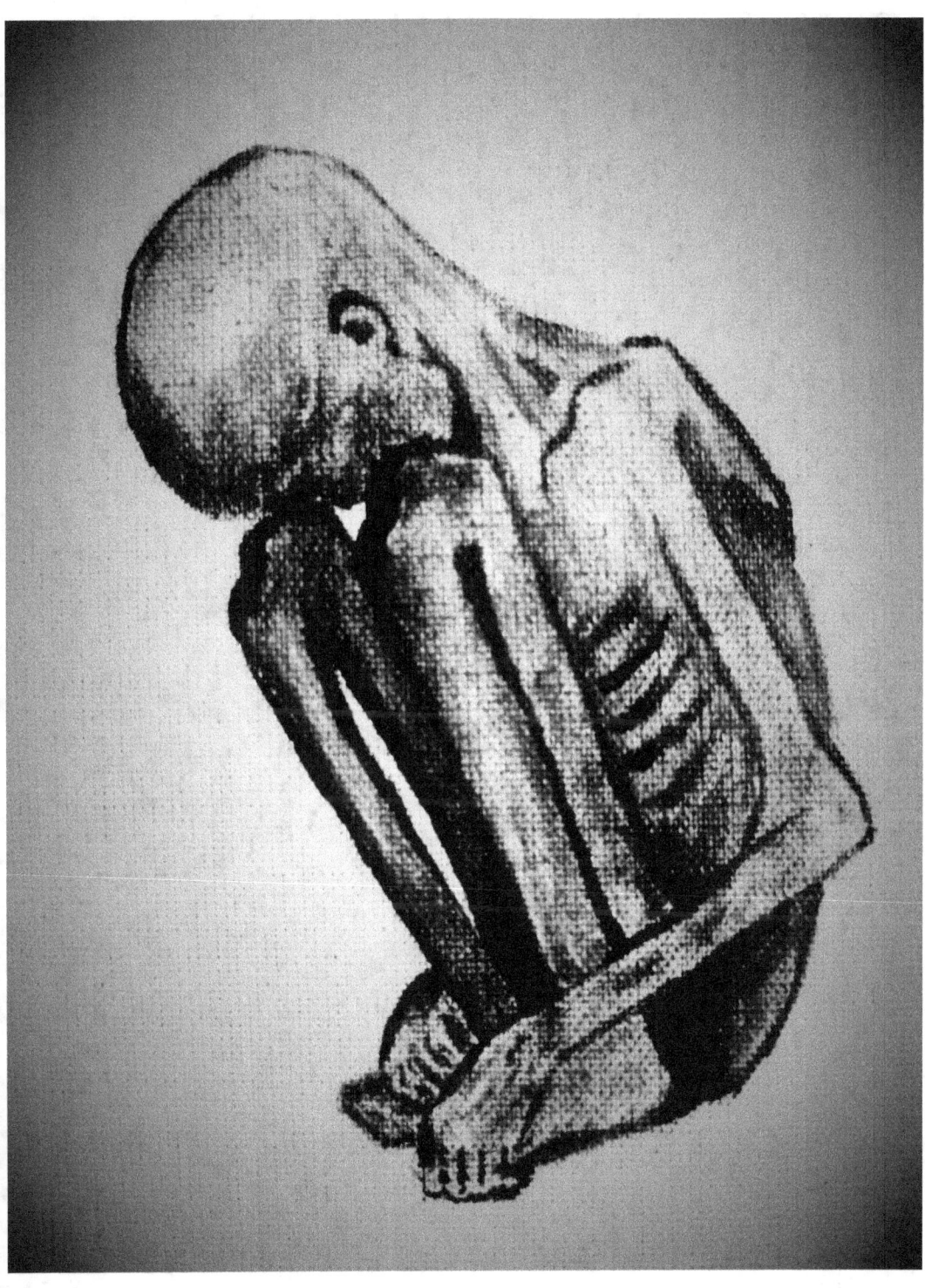

Seeds of Sorrow

There is no Planet B

Seeds of Hope

A Riddle of a Rhyme of Time

The seeds of ideas in time,
a different riddle of a rhyme.
What we seek must already be there,
the seeds of an idea must exist somewhere.
If you plant a seed in the ground
where before there's nothing to be found,
where does it come from?
If there was nothing there already waiting for it to become
then what?
Does the seed exist before the idea,
or the idea before the seed,
to what thought do you hold near?

We seem to want to get in touch with something that is already there,
but like any seed, it begins to grow in the dark,
it takes life from an unseen spark.
And when it begins to grow
it needs to be cared for and nurtured for its beauty to show.

Time is no guarantee of progression; that is plain to see,
one simply has to look at normal history,
the horrors we make now are the same as before.
Science and religion were meant to offer us another door.
Paths of time seem to collide, but the veil is down, so futures´ hide.
Ancients say "Eternity cuts through Time",
as if Time exists on different lines.

We may never know what we could become,
we may simply succumb,
but the idea may just be waiting for the seed to take root
and burst forth its glorious fruit.

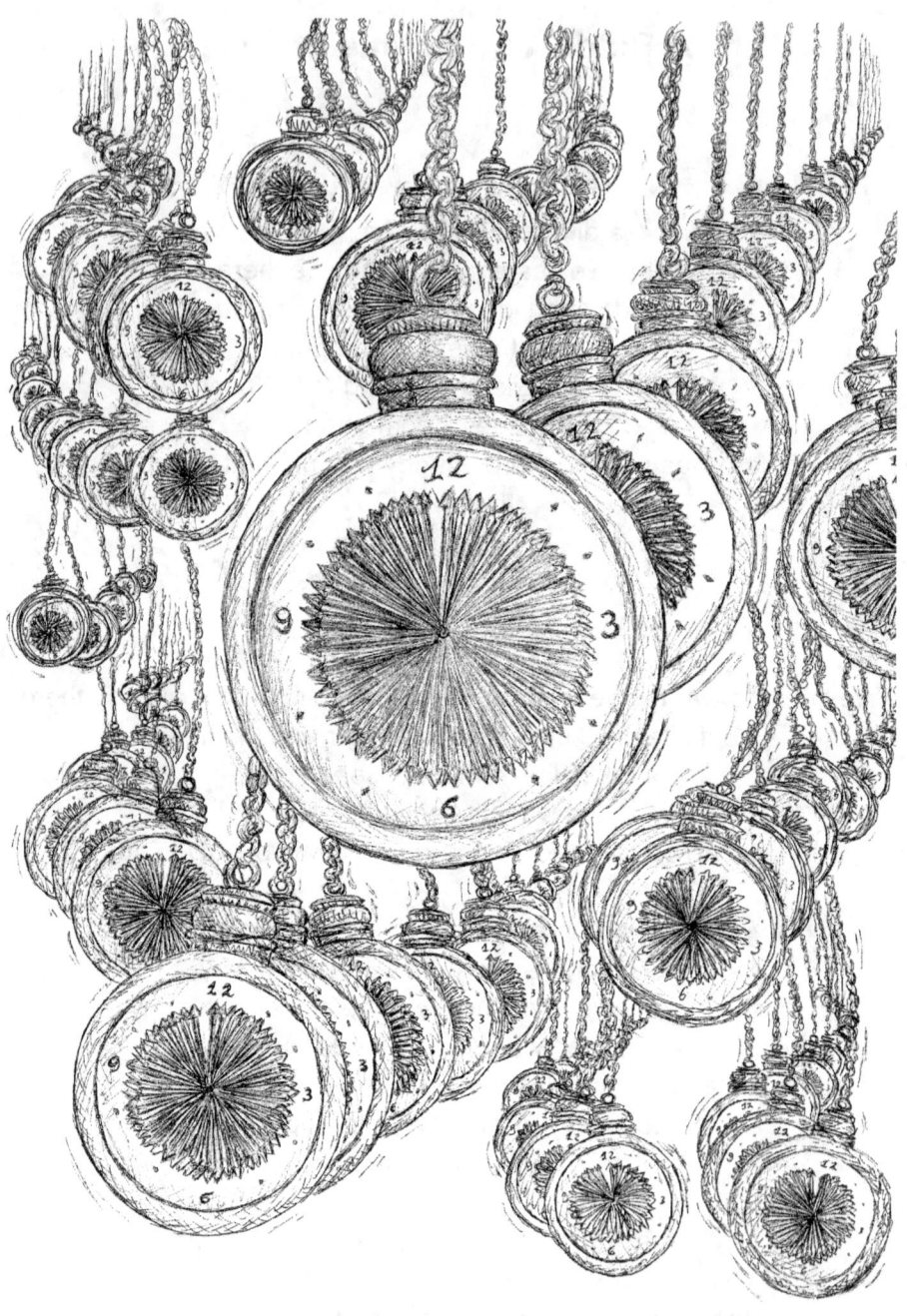

River of a Different Time

Social History class

The class had gathered, they were quiet and attentive, knowing they would learn things they needed to continue our way of living. It began with a silent greeting of awareness from the teacher.

She was pleased so many came today, this was basically voluntary history, and they had so much other work to do, although she would often include extra information on survival or sensory abilities to hold their interest, she knew it took their time away from other learnings. All the classes are involved in their own teaching and learning skills, they were still learning to teach each other. She had the information but she knew she must fade into the background and become increasingly unnecessary to them.

But this class was keen, always so many varied questions, their curiosity was inspiring, she always felt challenged to be truthful and present with this group, they have understood many things and their level of knowledge and external care to each other kept apace.

They were already teaching each other, she would miss them, but her new class will occupy her time soon, they were ready for their continuation class.

How did the slowing down happen?

Excellent, straight to the point, the follow up of a question from the last class, she loved this.

People brought a balance back.

Why were we out of balance?

Who can answer this for us all?

Another student said, it showed in the 'hollow-bilds' of the Histories, we were destroying our planet, consuming its resources at such a wasteful speed. It wasn't like today where things are more or less equalized. In those days just like most of human history, some people lived like kings others like paupers.

What were Kings? Asked another.

Do any of you remember about that part of history? Asked the teacher.

Yes, said another, they used to rule over all the people and lands where they lived.

Why?

The same student spoke; it was a part of the society and history of the Human race. That should be remembered, but only in so far that it never becomes repeated.

How long did the Kings rule for?

All their lives, then their son or daughter took over, that process continued for thousands of years.

That was a family controlled population?

Yes.

That's unfair.

To us, yes, said the teacher, but why is it unfair?

Another student said. Because inherited power means that that person has done nothing of merit to achieve that position, no self-qualities have developed to allow that person to rule over and make important decisions involved in running a society.

When did it stop?

When the world became Hot and the '99' took control. It was after the 'Age of Change'.

Did the Kings rule the world?

The Teacher asked if anyone remembered.

One of the students replied, for most of Human Time, but near the beginning of the 'Age of Change' large 'corporations' ruled the workings of the world for between one and two hundred years.

What happened to them?

Oh, they were nationalized or put out of business, the people who managed them were given a choice they could go to prison or share their wealth with the common people of the planet.

A balance had to be brought back, because the planet was on the edge of irreversible Climate Change. There was physical and financial violence and inequality all over the world from the ruling elite's policies.

It was a lot?

Yes, does anyone remember this information?

Yes, said another. The records are quite clear; it seems from the Histories that at the height of the inequality two billion people were in need of basic substances for survival. A billion people went to sleep every night hungry. A child died every few seconds of hunger. Much of the world was working as slave labour. Mostly women and people of a darker skin colour were treated as unequal and there were dozens of Wars, small and large all over the planet.

Some dozens of the richest people in many lands had more money than the rest of the population put together, and the laws that were set in motion meant it would never change, unless the people themselves did something about it.

They used to divide the people into classes. The poor, (those that had little money) were the lower class, those with some money and a reasonable chance of life were called the middle class, and generally those with lots of money were called the upper class. There were a few that were super-rich and then there were the many that were super-poor, they were the destitute with absolutely nothing, many people slept in the streets of the cities, begging for food or money for survival. With no social contact to people, these were often classed as the unwanted or the untouchables of society.

Why unwanted, why untouchable?

The teacher came in on this question to answer. Those were humans no-one wanted anything to do with. When other people saw them, they knew something was wrong, but it was a wrong difficult to face, it made people feel uncomfortable and like all realities that cause internal discomfort, we don't like to see them. Then we automatically find causes and reasons why things are as they are and console ourselves with all sorts of justifications. The end result being, we don't feel discomfort at seeing these contradictions within our society.

What were cars like to ride in?

Before answering the teacher reminded herself to speak slower now, she realized she had spoken to quickly, for the student had not been attentive to the implications of what was just said and his mind jumped all over the place. She must try to hold the level of attention more.

Well, you can try the simulator we have in the sensory information classes. It seems they were bumpy and dangerous, many died in them for they went to incredible speeds of movement. People made mistakes all the time, there were a lot of crashes.

And they all moved because of oil?

Mostly, they also had batteries, 'condensed energy storage', but during the destructive period they didn't seem to become too popular, except with people that didn't want to use oil anymore.

Someone asked why money was important?

Another student replied, it's where they placed their value of something, on external things.

True, the teacher said, but are there any other reasons?

Another student said, well yes, it was a form of exchanging commodities that was necessary for transactions between people, it was a 'common coin' I believe they called it.

Why don't we have money anymore?

The teacher answered. It isn't necessary. With the realization that most of life on our planet would cease within a few generations if we continued on the same path of self-destruction, it became obvious to most people that to bring back any sense of balance to the human race, a few certain ideas of human life must be changed.

The way the system had developed till then proved ineffectual, due to its inherent tendency to allow only a few to benefit at the expense of the many. In one way it was common sense to have a 'common coin', but the way it went had the effect of creating complete inequality all over the world. The accumulation of capital by the few always meant the opposite for the many, which was especially dangerous if those with much capital influenced political or social needs and ideas. This capital accumulation eventually led to those with less, most of the world, to call themselves the 99% and from the 99, the 'Heroes' arose.

It was transformed into a more human method of equal common exchange and mutual benefit. Would anyone like to add anything else?

Yes, well, I think we should mention that the Dramatic Climate Changes that happened, stemming from the increasing Global Warming of our planet, and that its causes and even existence had been denied for some years due to abnormal behaviour of those in positions of power. They followed their policies of inhumanly doings, with the action of conditioning much of humanity into accepting their tragic fate. Punishing people in all sorts of ways that had sought to help or inform others or work to change the disastrous situation.

Someone else asked how did they keep control?

The teacher spoke slowly. The powerful and constant influences of these *'Being-less' leaders continued through pretending things were other than what they were,* but not only. Wars were started and continued, often for personal and corporate financial interests, leading to controlling the resources of the world. That was achieved through force with wars of destruction and laws of manipulation.

It's as if the rich of the world had a party and only they got to eat at the table of the wealth of humanity. The poor ate the scrapes that were thrown to them. It had been that way for thousands of years in the main, but in these times of Dramatic Climate increasing disasters and effects, communication all over the world was instant, therefore policies implemented affected changes quickly, life became dramatically different for everyone in bad ways, except the rich.

Let's make time for a small reminding poem ladies and gentleman.

A small portion of people on a tiny planet out in space,
conditioned their species, called the human race.
Humans it seems were given a special role to recognize and be,
unfortunately mostly this we did not see,
until something happened that placed a problem in our face,
the likely extinction of our human race.

Will we ever go back to that way again?

As the teacher looked around the room she said. What do you think?

Unlikely, said someone, only if we let individuals have too much control and power. Unless people have a highly developed sense of 'being', power corrupts. Those who are not in a reasonable balance with themselves should never be allowed to become leaders. They become too one-sided, ruled by their careless or often negative and destructive thoughts, or their petty emotions of fleeting desires, their likes and dislikes, or they are led and controlled by their body's weaknesses.

Any and all of these 'being weakness' of 'being character' were always leading the power seekers of former times. We no longer allow that to happen, there are checks and controls in place.

Yes, said the teacher as she smiled, that sounds like a *very detailed* but accurate assessment of things.

How long will the planet continue to warm for?

We don't know, but it seems it will continue for thousands of years more, humanity will probably not make it. Survival would only be possible if our people of knowledge find practical and alternative solutions to counter the upward heating tendency.

But extinction is the normal for all species on Earth, none has survived forever, except perhaps the Crocodile, they seem to know something we don't. The students smiled at her. She continued, if we had learned how to communicate with the Dolphins perhaps we could have asked them, they used more of their brain capacity than we ever managed, but they died out along with the other intelligent species of the ocean due to the acid in the water.

But we don't burn fossil fuels anymore, so why is it still warming?

Let's open that question for everyone. Does anyone remember why?

Yes, said a student, it reached a tipping point, a point of no going back; our planet had recognised climate boundaries, I think it was nine in total and we were breaking them all, at high speed, being interconnected one thing affected another. All we managed to do with our 'reforms of world care policies' was to slow down the speed and effects just a little. It gave us more time, for the last few generations and the coming ones.

Do you think that we will always need our suits?

I think you know enough about your planet that you can answer that yourself, but yes, if that changed at all, which is about as likely as having snow today, it would not be for many generations yet. Your solar energized sensory survival suits allow your existence outside these walls now.

It's all you, the young, know of our world, but our planet has changed dramatically from the days when we made the world dark with oil and other chemicals that we dug out of our Mother Earth's body.

The other day we saw the 'hollow-bilds' of our histories, despite their technological advances they behaved in barbaric ways, it was full of bombs dropping on people killing them all; They called it 'Hell from above'. How was that stopped?

They had many names for the 'Sky-Death', 'Drone-War', 'Hell-Fire', names change over the years, like all language does. But the very idea of war changed from the New Government's policies in the transition of the 'Age of Change'.

As was said earlier, there was a reform of thinking; there was a choice at the time, revolution or reform. Revolutions always involve violence. All the histories that we know of include this, *but more interestingly, as you all know and have learned, one force will always bring a counter force*, so if violence is used to try to change something, violence will be used to try to stop it.

It's equal and it's opposite, that is a constant, discovered a long time ago, but never appreciated or understood deeply enough.

Some people did realize this deeper, we don't know who, for they were nameless. I think they were from the Sufi tradition of the ancient Teachings, but ask your teachers of the 'Contemplation classes' they will be more informed.

They realized what was needed was a revolution in thought, a reversal, in order to reform the policies of those in control and that it had to be Emotional, Personal, Collective, all at the same time, and come from the right place, people needed a common cause to rally around. They called it the 'EPC change', but you'll hear more of that in your other classes on social and personal responsibilities.

Let's use a reminding poem for the information.

One cause in common affected by many laws that were unjust,
we didn't need them, it wasn't a must.
These laws were an attack on the 'Human way',
they were changed, but not in a day,
it took the activation and participation of the young
to work without cessation.

Once it became clear that we lose all that we hold dear,
the young 'Heroes' rose with songs full of prose,
one sparked another, a fire was lit and it was bright.
The rulers tried to quell and suppress with all their might,
but that movement by the young we call the '99',
was for and by all the people who no longer wanted to stand in line –
to die.

They realized that this movement should never have one face,
for it was a movement of the Human Race,
and it was now - a race against time,
when they realized all would not be fine.

They had leaders that changed their roles,
their deaths were many, they fought for their souls.
There was much to distract and take their attention away,
after all it was a society conditioned over centuries to accept what the rich
and powerful did say.

There had always been movements to try to change the wrong,
but this movement was different,
it was the young and it was their song,
and they sung it in so many ways
all over the world, with different actions on different days.

They pressured the older generations to change,
the mums the dads, they were close and in range.
There was no child that went to school without knowing about the 'Golden
rule', one voice, one cause, we need just laws.

The rich and powerful had children too
and this was something this movement knew.
It was a movement to include all, for this moment would be Humanity's
dramatic climatic fall.
And it would not simply be a fall from grace;
it would be the fall of the 'Human Race'.

There was complete stillness, the teacher knew they were pondering the information and simultaneously sensing and feeling their body while being aware, a boy made a casual movement. The next question would come from him thought the teacher. The attention always fluctuates, but this was not what she taught, they learned about that in their 'Inner and outer sensation' classes. The question came.

And the stopping of the wars of destruction, the evil of the hell attacks from above? Sorry, but I don't understand how that was stopped.

Good, thought the teacher, let's take this deeper.

In short form, new governments made new laws.

In long form, it was the consequences of a natural follow through of a revolution in thought. Laws were changed to assure that companies no longer made any profits from the war machine. Privatized war profiteers were disbanded. The New Governments took control of many companies. They implemented laws to transform the poor and the unemployed of the world into a planetary workforce, for making wind, solar and water energy production for everywhere on the whole planet. They started to transform the transportation within their cities and around their countries.

They stopped breading cattle for mass consumption which was another source of methane gas as well as a technique called 'fracking' the Earth, which was also stopped. Millions of people went into working as farmers, the rural landscape was transformed. It took some years of transition. There were a few petro-states as well; those were countries that received much of their money from selling fossil fuels to the rest of the world. They were also changed. New materials and methods were used in building constructions for cities. The technology was already there, it was only the will power to achieve these changes that was missing.

There were obviously a lot of barriers put in place to try to stop these changes. War and poverty being two of the main distractions; populations kept occupied with War, Death, Starvation and Survival have very little interest in anything else. But you must remember, there was only one generation of time left to radically change the disastrous situation. One generation, almost nothing in regards to time. That's why we call these young people the 'Heroes'.

Everyone went to work; poverty levels disappeared within a short time. Everyone had enough food; the armies of the world went to work in real humanitarian ways, doing all sorts of projects. Building protections for coastal cities and moving some of them, organizing new places to live for the people of the islands that would first go under-water. Some countries were subsidized for a while; eventually it became the world effort we now know as the 'Age of Change'.

Gradually people were trained in multiple skills, producing a quality of life that enhanced their perception. After thousands of years they had one cause, regardless of national differences, they spoke as one voice. Before that had happened the hopeless state of all peoples was dramatic, it would normally have led to violent revolutions in which many more would have died, and only replaced one 'Being-less' leader with another.

But now the game had changed, and the rules of the game were different, no one leader held so much power and no-one kept their position of authority for long, this was a collective movement. It was all in transition out of necessity.

It was a process that had taken a little time to transform, but it had begun. Then one thing fell into harmony with another, it would take hours just to tell you some of the many actions of reform. It became like a fairy story, something magical had begun.

Surly not all the people way back then wanted that?

As was said before, there were many barriers, so no, not everybody wished for this, but they were in the minority. Normal life continued for many, survival necessities, violence didn't suddenly stop, but with a growing awareness of the planetary and personal situation, it just became less.

A real human education had begun and it had begun in the least technically advanced countries first, they called them third world countries, it seems to be another way of dividing people into a class system. To us they seemed to be the most advanced because of their social and moral qualities. The poor and indigenous of these lands fought in many ways for their rights, and Mother Earth's rights. These people were an inspiration to the poor in the richer countries of the world. Problems were still everywhere, but the magic had begun.

Those obstacles or barriers that the powerful tried to use to maintain their position didn't matter, eventually they were overcome. Scientific methods were put to work for the benefit of human needs and not for corporate profits. Good things began to happen. Global Warming was in their face, they formed one cause and one voice.

SEEDS: Saving Earth Every Day Somewhere

Policies were implemented that would assure that there would be no actions that would further endanger our planet. Trees were planted all over the world, and in their millions. Thousands went to work protecting the coral reefs; poor countries were being humanly helped instead of being un-humanly bombed. No oil or gas taken from the ground, only the bare minimum for a while.

Eventually all the evil actions against our planet ceased, when the new laws made sure that profit from sad evil action would no longer be possible. Many companies were closed, or transformed into positive, clean and reusable energy productions. Other laws were passed to make sure that companies could no longer buy or manipulate the governments.

People moved in a common direction in a common aim, survival of the Human Race.

They realized that there were two possible futures, two realities: the manipulated continuation of humans leading to civilization collapse and the end of the human race. Or face the reality of some of the most famous words in our history, 'to be or not to be', that was and is the question.

The challenge in that question is always new, it's the response that is old. We needed a new response, a common sense, a common direction, a new way of being here on this planet, an ever present factor that reminds us why we now do what we do. That is our 'reminding factor' that gives us the power to continue to be. Your education is as complete and as well rounded and balanced as we can make it, in order to have a society of well-adjusted emotionally stable, adaptable, intelligent young people, able to cope and deal with the necessities of our now desperate but balanced existence on an unbalanced planet.

Humanity had followed the history of the path of violence for so long, it was as if it would never change, or it would destroy itself in barbarism or nuclear war. The climate threat was the shock that was necessary for a change to embark on a new direction of human living possibilities.

Human compassion was the unseen spark of conscience that arose in its unquenchable flame – across humanity – giving untold power to the real meaning of the name – 'wise-man'.

Who invented our 'Gliding Boards'?

In every class I've ever taught someone always asks that. When I was your age it was me, actually the answer is interesting. No-one knows, the name was not given, one of the later generation after the 'Age of Change', we don't know who exactly, it was a girl, she turned the technology over to be freely used without wanting credit to her name, there isn't even a hollow-bild, she wanted no recognition, it seems she was soaked in the lore and stories of the 'Heroes'.

That was one of the big turning points of the movement of transportation change. Self-renewing, solar powered gliding boards, everybody loved that. There was no going back after that.

And the long stage travel to the other side of the planet?

It was slowed down and phased out for many people for a while until the technology was able to supply non-atmospheric damaging planes. After that there was no real problem with that anymore.

Who invented our suits?

Again a girl from one of the later generations, again we don't know her name, by that time no-one needed or wanted fame. The story is she simply wanted to work in the mountains and study the atmospheric changes for helping humanity to adapt to what was happening.

The design is so perfect it's never been changed since the first one.

Did many die in the transition?

Would someone else care to answer this question, some of you have studied this?

Yes, said a student. In the beginning, but not anywhere near as how many were dying before, which was all over the planet from wars, disease and starvation.

For instance, at the height of their insanity, there were 25 wars large and small all over the planet. One child every minute died of a disease called malaria, which was curable; 5 thousand children died every day of starvation in a world of plenty. One billion went to sleep every night hungry.

Hundreds of thousands died regularly in their wars of conquest and plunder in search and control of oil and natural resources. In the African countries millions died in the control over minerals for the technologically advanced societies. Those in world power were guiding the general populations into reverting back to extreme levels of poverty of previous times, many were made homeless and at the same time still encouraging those that could, to consume more. Their society of consumption knew no bounds.

Before the 'Age of Change', it could have been called the age of consumption; it would have needed five or six more planets to sustain the unnecessary consumption of the people of some countries.

Why did it take so long for the Heroes to rise?

Okay, on this point I would like to give you a few minutes to talk amongst yourself about this, then, please someone speak for you to give an answer to the whole class.

After a few minutes one of the students began to speak.

It seems the structure of the richer societies had conditioned its people in uncaring ways, and simultaneously conditioned them to become immersed in inane trivia instead of the necessities of life. The young and old alike were occupied with 'things' not needed for the real concerns of living. When people were so busy with their pastimes they had the illusion of living. Their attention was consistently deflected away from things of importance, instead of being cultivated into normal human care, compassion and participation.

Okay, said the teacher, but I'd like to add to that, that what people were up against, we in this society cannot really know, we haven't lived through that, no matter what you see in the 'hollow-bilds' of the histories.

These points of inane trivia and pastimes that you mention, as true as that was for many, can easily be looked upon as a form of temporary escape from the pressures of daily life and existence, whether that be watching what they called movies or consuming drugs or alcohol.

It's important to emotionally recognize and empathize with the fact that the majority of people were having trouble surviving, getting enough food to feed their family, worried about their children's health and the basic cost of survival in whatever country they lived.

So dear people don't be judgmental on this, we have no right to be. Our own society is not free of problems, and how we live now is intrinsically connected to what they went through, suffered, and overcame.

To fully comprehend the subliminal manipulation techniques that were conducted on peoples since early childhood and continuing through all stages of their life is an immense study. For instance, to be conditioned to like your local sports team, a brand of some product. In foods, with fake flavours to make you want more, embedded messages in advertising, to follow trends or fashions that make you feel whatever they wanted you to feel. With colours, shapes, ideas to appeal to certain age groups or the different sexes.

To condition men and women into accepting certain roles psychologically, starting in childhood education and never stopping. To condition people to accept levels of violence and kill others and also to train people through media to accept that as normal behaviour, these and a thousand and one other things we don't have time to mention. The invisible chains of this hypnotism were almost unbreakable, another reason as to why they were called the 'Heroes'.

You and I and all here, simply don't have that anymore, we have never experienced it, for that we should be thankful. There was silence for a while after that information had time to penetrate.

How did they choose the activities to work on way back then?

They didn't choose really, they reacted out of necessity. Certain structures for the society were simply creating and maintaining the disastrous situation. Mainly their use and abuse of their monetary system that they lived under, it seems to be that everything stemmed from that.

They had forms of business that simply did not contribute to the structure and betterment of society, some of these were 'speculative', in the sense that they tried to 'predict the future', which from a normal social sense was absurd. Since their scientists quite clearly explained what the future had in store, a rapidly heating planet.

Someone defined the principle as M-C-M, standing for Money-Commodities-Money; it's a whole subject in itself that we won't go into in this class as we don't use it anymore. A monetary system in itself is not bad or wrong, but it's like anything in life, it was in the way it was put to use. Things can be used in beneficial and constructive ways for the benefit of the many or its opposite; the power seekers choose the opposite.

It's interesting to note that through time it changed several times and assumed the wording of Mad-Capitalist-Monster, and even later into Mad-Carbon-Monster, the one I really like myself was, Municipal-Common sense-Moralities, but, back to the actual activities.

Activities in the past included building cities with new materials, relocating costal populations. Methods of transportation changed and especially food transportation. At the time of the Heroes, most of the food on the planet travelled half around it, if not all the way before arriving at its destination.

Why?

It's complicated, but basically companies made more money that way. This financial structure simply failed to fulfil genuine social requirements and responsibilities.

The amount of waste in non-reusable materials was immense. For instance they had 300 million tons of plastic each year that they simply dumped in the ocean or lands or burned into the atmosphere.

When was the last time humans used plastic?

I'm not sure, maybe a hundred and fifty years. Does anyone know any different? No?

Well anyway, food production was returned back into the hands of farmers, food grown and cultured where it was eaten, small sized farming by rural workers came back and was reintroduced and millions were trained in the older arts of growing food. Millions moved back into the countryside to work the Earth with a combination of new technology and old ideas, minus the poisons. Collective land rights became the normal.

Didn't the people have a harder life because of that?

It depends on how you look at that. At the time of the Heroes which was the praecipe of Climate Change for all Earth, one third of the people of the planet lived in cities and were living in poverty and slums, which means the worst living conditions possible. So moving to the countryside to work the lands again was simply reversing the trend that had been occurring for the previous two hundred years or so.

Families grew together again in connected ways that were basically destroyed due to coming to work in cities, in factories or whatever else they tried to do to survive, which had been happening all that time.

The New Governments utilized the northern parts of the world for wind and water power, and at the same time transforming the southern warm sun drenched lands into solar power generating areas. Vast, mostly uninhabited land mass was converted. Eventually the combination of energies supplied the world; countries became equalized through this supply and request effect.

Was this at the same time as we lost most of the animal and insect species?

That came a bit later I think, said the teacher, at the time I'm thinking of now, the planet was losing about a thousand species a week, over half the population in the oceans were gone from over fishing or dead from poisons. This was a disaster. Actions were taken to try to reverse this horrendous fact. Where possible, animals, fish and insects were bred and reintroduced. People went to work in trying to restore these dying populations; this was difficult in the oceans due to them becoming more acidic. On land, forests and ecology were simply devastated. None the less efforts were made.

What about the diversity of the peoples?

Cultural diversity, hand in hand with solidarity of all peoples was encouraged and educated as a primary; as this movement grew, it needed and heeded everyone.

This was a world social necessity, to have a participating population involved in social, economic and moral issues, not only of personal survival and conduct, but of world maintenance. The system at the time of the 'Age of Change' was maintaining and increasing the path towards civilization collapse and Global destruction.

For the countries that had been kept poor and under privileged through domination, their water, food and transportation systems were updated with solar and wind power. Many ideas were exchanged between peoples at this time regarding food growth and supplies. Also education became a Top priority.

They had what were called democracies at this time, but they were intrinsically connected to their monetary system. In fact, it was a very profitable business for the few, and their wars of society maintenance were normally a form of international destructive business. Someone named that method SAD, Society And Democracy. And being so connected, someone else in fun changed it later to MAD - Money And Democracy, borrowed from the Nuclear aphorism Mutually Assured Destruction.

Speaking of which, atomics were simply banned due to realizing the obvious absurdity of having them in the first place. With the problems between the countries not everything went peacefully at first, but eventually all complied. There were difficulties and much struggling for a while, but the cause and the voice were strong, for the calls were many, and it was a social, structural and collective change of all societies.

What did they do with their soldiers?

Would anyone care to answer this question for you all?

Yes, said another, many of these people had a great many other talents that were put to use in building, engineering, aviation, their knowledge of lands and the ocean, many specialized, not all were warriors, over time they were all put to good use, many had become disillusioned with their morally corrupt leaders and some became the young 'Heroes' themselves.

I saw that people used to carry guns around or have them in their homes even when they weren't soldiers.

Yes, that's true.

Why did they do that?

For some it was how they felt safe, it was their protection, for others it was a sense of power, to achieve aims through violence or the threat of it.

Was that difficult for them to change?

I don't know, probably, it's reported that when those in positions of power were all changed, the new interim leaders simply made laws banning weapons.

By then they had the technology to know when people had killer weapons, the laws were passed. That and they de-militarized the police force, which was itself a very good thing, for at the time it was being transformed into an army. After that, if people had unresolved issues they could freely demonstrate again without fear of physical danger from their government.

Will the weather patterns we have now ever change?

The Teacher was silent and contained her attention for a moment, she was sorry she had to say what she was about to. This question comes to all eventually, but it's something we grow up with, it's how we relate to necessity, by knowing the truth of the situation we are in. None the less it's always asked in one of the classes.

As much as I would like to be able to tell you different, no, unfortunately it will only increase. Storms, hurricanes and floods of immense power destroying all in their path, it's simply too hot to work or live outside without our suits. It seems we and the coming generations will always now have the beautiful but deadly 'sky-art' of lightning strikes around many parts of the planet. The possibility of growing food in the old ways has long disappeared, so we will have to rely on our technology. The energy we have now is unending but causes no harm to our planet. Parts of our world become desert. In the struggle for drinkable water our new methods help but will always be a haunting reminder.

Also unfortunately, as you all know the acid oceans rise all the time that is now a constant, that's why we have many mountain cities. Within the times of the 'Age of Change' we lost many millions of people due to being too slow to implement the changes required. Our changes were good and for the betterment of all humanity, but none the less we only slowed down the devastation. Tragically, as well as much human life, we lost almost all animal life on the planet. The Global Warming came and is still changing this planet, but the temperatures that we are heading towards, well, sadly for us, life as we know it does not exist at that level. We simply don't know how long we have.

We're still learning ladies and gentlemen. There was and always is Hope. As you know Having Only Positive Emotions is not always possible, it's not a constant, but it's to boldly aspire to that, combined with having empathy for others, to consider the difficulties that others have, which gives us the strength we need to continue.

Recently I was reminded of a poem and teaching idea that my great grandmother wrote. In her later years she came back here to lead social history and contemplation classes. I thought I'd share it with you as it's relevant.

The Teaching Suggestion

History taught in the past was often only a history of crime, usually manipulated according those in control, so it became a distorted mirror of history. Since the 'Age of Change' our social history classes are of efforts, not of wars and crimes, but of actions taken to learn from, contemplate, if necessary adapt. Our aim is to help the continued growth of our culture. This involves personal observations and questions to attend to needs and necessities as they arise for personal human growth.

Social and personal contemplation is not merely to think; it is to bring your-self more into contact with the present moment, in order to become collected in oneself and less scattered. One of the tools we use is self-sensing.

History was taught in the past to tell a truth that didn't last.
Facts were altered to suit the needs
of those in control of policy creeds.
In our social history classes now,
we try to do it differently somehow.
We all have a need and we too have a creed.
For we need to empathize with others of our race
as our planet heats at a deadly pace.

You will discover as you learn,
that mostly you are our concern,
so we invest in you the young,
to sing a song that must be sung,
the Song of Hope.

Thank you for your questions and answers, your active participation and of course as always, your attention, our time is over for today. See you tomorrow.

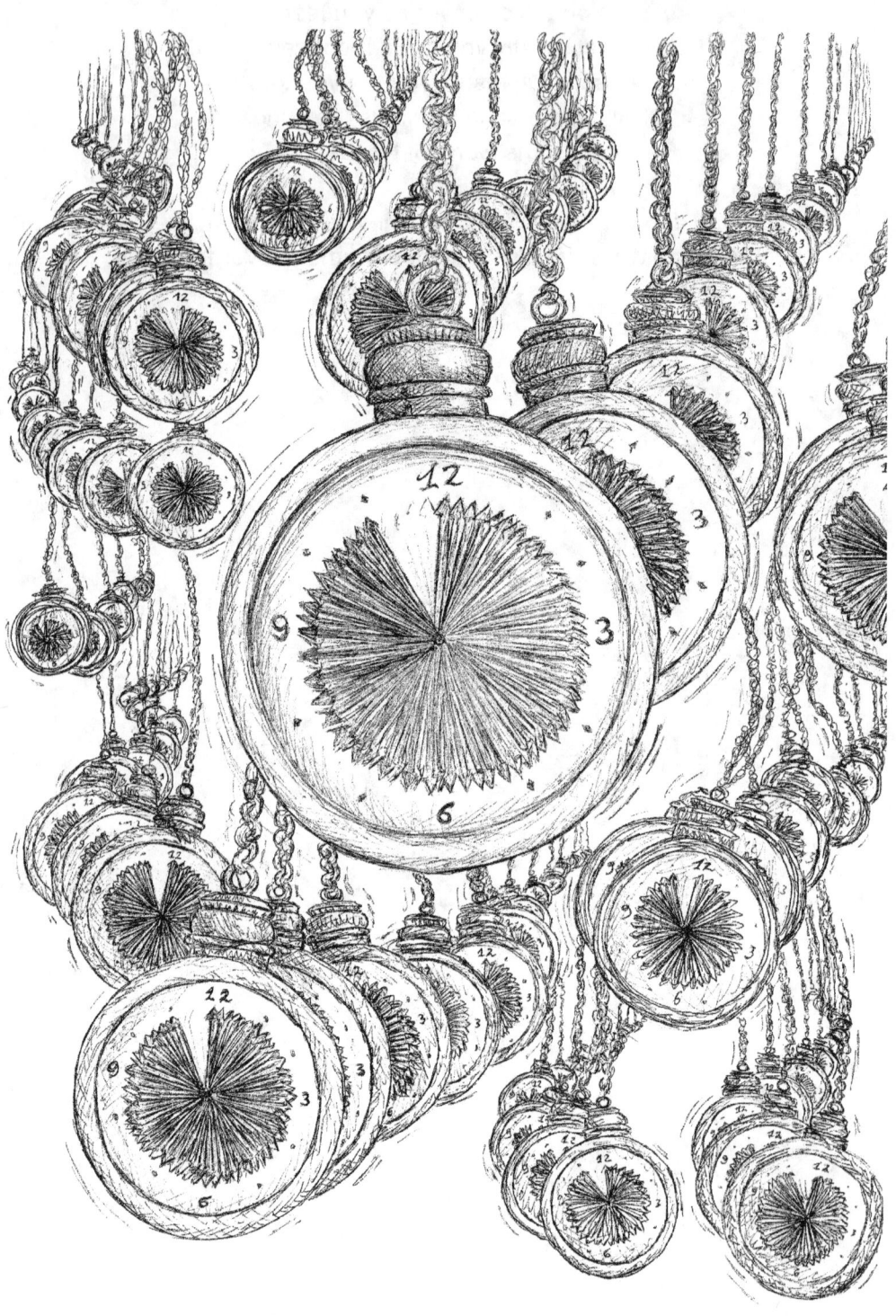

A long time ago

The Culture of Contemplation

The girl was on her way to the history class, she was keen on those classes, she tried never to miss any, and they got to look at all sorts of things from the captured moments of the 'hollow-bilds' of History.

She had just left the 'class of contemplation', where she was taught as always about thinking and feeling at the same time while sensing. It was difficult to maintain that, but her teachers helped, they said there was improvement and reminded her that it was a life-long practice.

They had been working on having 'voluntary sensations' from one of the old Teachings which taught that 'Inner sensation' normally, only came through an 'emotional blow like great sorrow or danger'.

This involved the 'sensing being present' exercises, which always had the effect on her of 'Being there' more. It was something that the young 'Heroes' of the 'Age of Change' had tried to encourage with each other, a stunning achievement in itself way back then.

Some of her friends weren't as interested as she was and yet others wanted to become like the 'Heroes' of 'The Age of Change'. They had read about the 'Heroes' and some of the actions they started, those who wanted to save the world: she covered many of their works they had begun.

She felt privileged to be a part of this study, this phase of human development. Life had changed already very much since her parents were born. So many things were in transition times, they were educated about the world that was and never should be allowed again.

It no longer would, there were checks and balances in place to ensure the transition would continue when the initial impulse faded, as they were taught that it would. The world of nature never moved in straight lines, which included movements and ideas that people tried to implement. This had been long understood.

She recounted one of the 'reminding poems' while she sensed where she was.

The Heroes rose to save the world,
it was the young, no longer were they curtailed,
despite the difficulties that were placed in their path,
they raised their voice against this awesome wrath.

The wrath of the rich and powerful, whose weapons were many
and could see inside the young's head,
they could observe their every action for a calling to halt,
their 'Being-less leaders' merciless assault,
on the human race at a deadly pace.

The young became the Heroes of ancient past;
they raised their voice eventually at last.

The Heroes came in every land; they had come to understand
that together they could work for change,
in a world of possibilities that was new and strange.

They came to realise that their leaders were dead,
they operated only from their head,
they controlled policy and many laws did make,
they didn't care that all human life was at stake.
Their PR had cancelled the young,
and for every new generation there was a different song to be sung, but the
play was always the same, 'buy our stuff, join our game.'

'You too can rise to the rich,
if you treat anyone and anything like your bitch,
tread upon and do not care about humanity deep in there,
in you deep inside. Don't worry about others if you're okay,
we'll give you a vote but control what you say.
If we don't like it, we can hear, for to us you're always near.
With the tools of our trade, we can have you slayed.'
The young woke up to the fact they had no choice,
the Heroes began to find their voice.

To work, to change, to wake others to this call,
it needed the participation of one and all.
There was much to be done,
but it was one generation of time left or a burning sun.

Social History Class

The class began in silence, the teacher soaked in the presence of so many eager students. The girl sat with the others, all were sensing themselves being there; aware of herself within the group, she knew the others would be doing the same, not always possible, failure in this exercise of Presence was inevitable, but as one of her teachers told her, 'that doesn't matter; seeing that often and making the effort to be Present is the important thing.' 'A thousand times', as one of the most ancient poets had said.

The first question came from her friend who wanted to work with ocean studies. Why the name 'The Heroes' and not another name?

The teacher began slowly, well, there were two reasons; the first is connected to the fact that there was one generation of chance left for change, to reverse the policies of the rich and powerful and the ongoing cultivated tendencies of the Human Race. Would anyone like to add to this?

Yes, said one of the students. It needed a collective movement, but that wouldn't happen unless people were emotionally engaged. They needed to be informed, to awaken their emotions which had been for quite some time commercially manipulated to be wasted on trivia or in daily survival.

In a sense people had to feel rage and sorrow about the interconnected injustices that were taking place. So the name 'Heroes' was given to the young participants of the '99' movement for their aim was Helping-Everyone-Rise-Over-Every-Society.

It needed to be a collective movement and these young people were rising against the established powers, a well-oiled structure, that had access to intelligence about all peoples of the world, all the time. The young and the old were monitored and often manipulated in many ways. So to attempt to rise against such an oppressive power, there is no other name to give except 'Hero'.

Yes, good, that's a pretty comprehensive answer, said the teacher. The second reason comes from way back at the beginning of western culture, some of you will know this of course, but some not. A large part of the culture of the western world at the 'Age of Change' came from Ancient Greeks, from their laws and teachings and from their myths and legends, which were also forms of passing information on through time, of ideas, beliefs and methods, of relating to the world we live in.

It's also important to remember that the culture we have now is a combination of all cultures and teachings that were inspirational for different peoples at the 'Age of Change'. The times and necessities required bridges of understanding to be built between nations.

Would anyone else like to continue the answer?

Yes. The girl spoke now. I'd like to connect the culture and myth aspects. The Ancient Greeks had different names for certain types of people, and one of those names was the 'Heroes', the 'Heroes' were special. Legends arose around their stories, at some point they were called the 'Children born of the Gods', I feel this was a distorted idea, but more important, was the incipient idea, that the qualities and possibilities of the 'Hero' lay dormant or buried within every Human born on Earth, which of course connects the ideas in all major Teachings as well.

Yes, good, said the teacher, that quality was often covered over or rather people were asleep to it, and it had to be awakened in order to respond to that request, for it is a request, and no easy task. In your other classes, you are taught more on this subject as you know, so I won't spend much longer on this point.

Instead I'd like you to imagine the difficulties of the young 'Heroes' at the 'Age of Change', it was the praecipe of Climate Change, their difficulties and barriers were immense.

They had managed to a degree to awaken the Hero within themselves, and further tried to awaken the Hero in all. The world waited as if in breathless silence, soon that silence would turn into a roar of rage and sorrow and awaken all to the call.

Could you talk some more of the problems that they were up against?

Sure, but let's look on it from a different perspective than how we've spoken about this before.

There were two different but connected problems. One problem was that some people sought to have power over others. And the second problem was that people were conditioned in their culture to seek fame. Let's speak about fame first. Seeking fame meant that people spent their time and energy in trying to get attention of some sort, and also to film it for the world to see on their different media communication methods. It distracted them and kept them occupied.

A pupil said, but we watched some of the histories the other day and they were really funny and entertaining, I can see why people would want to watch and even make them. Why do we talk about it as if it's negative?

The teacher replied, it's not a negative thing at all actually, and yes many are fun to watch, but that's part of the problem, 'entertainment' means 'to amuse or distract attention'. At the time of the 'Age of Change' it was like having a party while the house is on fire.

The teacher added, that mostly people knew this, but like many things we know of but do not understand deeply enough, which is where things lead to. And in this case it led many people in most lands all over the world to be occupied with trivial entertainment.

Large companies and those in power liked and used this very cultivated aspect of society to their benefit, encouraging populations in more of the same, same but different.

The children from an early age were being targeted and trained to be just like the machines they were using, and conditioned in ways that they felt no need to ever question these mind numbing activities; in part, it was what we call *acceptance through attraction.* Would anyone like to add to this?

Yes, said the girl, just to be clear. Seeking recognition for one's self-worth when in the early growing stage of life is a necessary aspect of normal human development. To feel self-worth and have meaning for living is extremely important. The love, care, appreciation and acknowledgment of your unique individuality from your parents or elders here is necessary. But as we age and develop, *seeking recognition of uniqueness can lead into all sorts of strange behaviour.*

Very good, said the teacher, yes this is something that should always be remembered.

The girl continued. People at the time of the 'Age of Change' recognized that the life they were living was being manipulated through multiple methods of distraction and attraction. One of the ways they described it themselves was 'behavioural engineering' within education and all of society itself, guiding them towards the path of sameness, of uniform, a society with the embedded illusion of freedom under surveyed control, and due to the disastrous effects of predatory capitalism on the planet's ecology, also heading on a speeding train towards destruction and barbarism.

The teacher said that this is an important point, so can anyone repeat it in a different way.

Another girl answered. Occupying a society with anything and everything of trivial interest would stop them questioning about things of real value. About world concerns in general and in the ultimate case Anthropogenic Global Warming.

Good, said the teacher. Let's speak about another aspect now. She continued. Through trying to find better principles to live by, it was realised by some that all attempts, all efforts to ameliorate human existence *based only* on external changes will in the end fail, since mankind would essentially remain the same, the same kind of man. But it was also realised that as an individual he could change, and this is how we try to educate our children in these days and have done so now for a long time.

Although we live collectively, we each must try to recognize and remain unique and individual in our existence, and that there was and is something to awaken and cultivate in humans, compassion and empathy, which led us to the ideas we now work with about having a balanced existence on a personal and collective level.

The examples of manipulated distractions are many, the effects disastrous for any meaningful social or personal progress. All of these causes and more were the haunting background reasons as to why a change was necessary. This path which humanity was on had led us to where species extinction was imminent; it was and still is a planetary emergency.

Now in regards to the other problem, one of power seekers, power seeking, can as we all know, often lead to tendencies of domination of individuals or societies. When this is not checked, it encourages people to indulge in their weaknesses. When we allow people with these weaknesses of character to be in positions of power, they would manipulate others and not care of the consequences of their actions. That means their decisions affect millions if not billions of poor souls all over the planet in disastrous ways, not only causing but continuing the 'ecocide' of our planet.

In other words, these are people who have not matured as humans can and should never be leading a society. No matter how serious, attractive, well spoken, intelligent, pleasant or strong in personality people may seem on the outside, their psychology, their inside, may be that of the opposite, distorted, weak, full of jealousies and insecurities, envious of others, the list of the negatives unfortunately is endless.

This is why we have often quoted one of the most ancient of Teachers that we have records of. - When Plato made the observation, which is as relevant today as it was when he said it, that what we need are 'Teachers of Being'. It was one of the many instructions for the continued education of humanity, in the past, sadly often ignored or simply not understood deeply enough.

So having people in positions of power that lacked compassion and empathy and were prone to weakness in their vanities was a danger, and there is another danger, always there. – It was mentioned briefly in passing, which you will know more of from your other classes. As any civilization disintegrates; man falls down into a level of violence and inhumanity which becomes our tragic and horrendous fate. What we have gained in our humanity so far holds us together; it keeps us away from the forces of barbarism which has been the fate of many cultures. Cultures have been established and for a time hold a level and even try to go beyond what they have already achieved, in order to begin again another culture in another part of the world when the pendulum swings and the 'forces of barbarism' and destruction hold sway.

On this path of humanity, this river of time that we go through, we struggle against the current, and the current always heads towards barbarism. Our human race is different than other sentient beings; but our possibilities are not guaranteed to be achieved. Our culture now has not had time enough to develop to its full potential, and it seems most likely that we will be the last culture on this planet.

The young of the '99', eventually *in their own way,* came to realize this and used their awareness of the situation as a tool for social transformation. Turning away from the direction and idea of fame or power as they gradually came into contact with deeper and more meaningful parts of themselves, which was connected to realizing the difficulties and tragedy of their social and world structure that were amongst other problems leading them to having a warming planet.

This was a major turning point; recognizing the terror of the situation they were in.

*   *   *

What else happened when that changed?

Violence against women who are the 'Mothers of our Race' and children who are the 'Hopes for our future' lessened and stopped. Patriarchy and Racism in general started on a river of change. Slave labour ceased, many innocents were released from unnecessary incarceration in prisons. All political representatives were replaced by common consensus, locally organized.

Power was never again allowed to get out of control or given to a small group of individuals with a dominance of character but with a weakness of being.

You see; when you take away the possibility of profit from the enslavement and abuse of others, much of these wrong and plainly evil actions, by necessity, fade as well. Taking away power and profit is what was called a 'game changer'.

Of course it's all a bit more complicated than that due to weaknesses of character in certain persons. The rich and powerful did not want their status quo upset, *their balance of power*, when in reality their sense of balance had unbalanced the planet, but the basic idea was there. Changing and adapting to circumstances as time passed.

After taking the power away from the largest of organizations and corporations through changing the laws and nationalizing them, their riches and purpose were directed into beneficial aims for humanity. Would anyone like to talk about that?

Yes, said the boy next to her, this had many carry on effects, food production, transportation and packaging all had to be changed. Environmentally clean transportation within cities became the normal. Products that were produced had no more a shortened 'End of Life' expectancy; things were made to last a bit longer reducing waste throughout the world. No more privatization of life necessities like water was allowed, all these actions and many more were happening throughout the world.

They had made radical transformations of their social and economic interactions between countries, for they were at the tipping point of no return of 'Irreversible Climate Change'.

A couple of the main Ideas of the 'Age of Change' were that fossil fuels must stay in the ground and the financial system they called capitalism must change, and the different societies had to deal with the effects of that, which were obviously dramatic, but as they came to realize, not as dramatic as a rapidly warming planet.

The common purpose of saving the planet to allow for Human and all other forms of species to continue to live on Earth became the cornerstone upon which people stood. And as we already know, that meant the social and economic systems should have the qualities of equal participation in decision making at all levels, beginning locally in consensus then through representation in larger groups.

Yes, that all sounds well thought out, just another thought to add to that. *After a while it was no longer about the prevention of climate disasters,* like increasingly powerful hurricanes coming from warming seas, flooding's, droughts, losing the coastal cities due to rising oceans, dead zones in the increasingly acidic seas due to absorbing large amounts of carbon, and of course, the inevitable Heat, *but about surviving them and dealing with the changing 'necessities' as they occurred.*

The teacher ended the class with a few questions that everyone should try to contribute in some way; as usual she left it up to them to work out the details.

Out of our collective world needs and from the dreams and aspirations of the heroes of the 'Age of Change' or before, what have we failed to achieve, as yet? What can we still improve in our society in the present? What will we need to continue in the coming future? How can we get there? What problems will we come up against as we try to make more changes?

The girl left the class as always stunned at the courage and ingenuity of the young 'Heroes' who risked so much, and some of their images still on the 'hollow-bilds' for all to see and be encouraged and inspired.

She was studying to work on one of the power mountains where the combinations of wind and solar were most strong. Her best friend had opted for wind and ocean work, but she herself really wanted to live in the mountains, where she came from, she had spent so much time in this training city, she wanted back to the mountains where she felt herself more at peace. If she lived long enough she would return here to teach, if she could, she liked the social history classes.

She loved the mountains but it was too hot to work outside during the day without protection anymore. In her BIT classes (Bio-Informed-Textiles) she had been working on a new idea for a thermo suit that would protect and sustain her working outside. If she completed that she could live in the mountains for some years. She'd be studying the atmospheric changes, developing the energy and food systems needed to sustain her people. It would also allow her people to move around easier and planetary existence would be more bearable outside the protection domes that were going up all over the world. She sung a reminding poem that had inspired her.

The young Heroes of the world did rise,
they began to open each other's eyes
they no longer toed the line,
realizing their world would no longer be fine.

Together they formed their own sacred band,
and sacred it is, for that is what it is to understand,
that there is more to life than having money, power and control,
and that the rich had sold something that belonged to all,
a planet, that we all need, the rich, they let it bleed.

The Heroes of the modern world were no longer individual
and a p a r t, they made a movement and it did start,
to change the tide and roll back the wave,
to this one movement and this one cause,
their time and life they gave.
The young became the Heroes, for planet Earth to save.

An idea did start;
who could do the most for life, for it was not a dying Art.
To wake each other with their call, not one or a few, but all,
a generation left to try, they would do it or they would die.

Movements took place to serve the human race;
they were everywhere inspired, they had a cause.
No more of the rich and their selfish laws,
'all for me and none for you',
the young Heroes sung something new.

Injustices were fought, those who started wars must be brought
to seeing it's not the human way to continue in this modern climate day,
exploitation of the world became the past,
the old ways they shouldn't last.

This is a world of young Heroes all,
we have a voice and a call and our world needs us all.
Our call is soft and one of care, Saving Our Future today -
Can Always Remember Earth - some way.

She made the decision, she must finish the suit, it would be composed of the smallest flexible solar panels ever made, based on the self-renewing technology that had been developed, it would include a system of capturing and re-distilling the body fluids, along with expansion and contraction methods for the dramatic changes between day and night, and the coming future of course. Although she used the artificial intelligence methods of constructing, it would be independent of technology once in existence, self-regulating once in action. In her mind she called it the 'Triple-s', the sensory survival suit, for in essence that's what it would be.

Necessary for the future, people will need them, otherwise it would be life underground or always enclosed and that was unthinkable.

If only they had reacted sooner in the past, we would have been ready for all of these changes, but at least that generation of young Heroes finally took action against the corrupt, for that she was thankful. Human life had changed for the better.

Not the heat of the planet of course, but at least it wasn't as bad as it could have been, yet, and society was progressing in different ways, the 'Teachings' of old were being lived, no more silliness of the careless, cruel and selfish times of Human history, but how much time was left, no-one really knew. She quietly said another reminding poem.

Heroes they had all become, the story of the sacred young,
for it's where they discovered to be true,
'we can try something new,
to rule the world with a 'common sense'
and 'common rights' to dispense.
The rich with their destructive ways should not rule in these days.'

A policy of 'One world' came to pass,
Climate Change was the rallying mast.
The Heroes were mobilized to act,
with each other they made a pact,
'save the world, it's all we've got,
no longer will we be sold or bought,
nor observed in our every move.

The powerful, the rich, they disapprove;
it's their attitude that must improve,
there should be no rich or class in our new days.'
These were the words that were said,
as the balancing laws were made and read.

They did not fight the governments of incipient repression where the police
were heading way out of control,
no; they turned to their mothers and fathers,
who made that army whole,
and convinced one and all to turn back,
and slow down our planet on its speeding track.

With a generation left to change,
desperate measures were brought in range.
Women, mothers, daughters, all, fought for a human right,
they brought their baring into the light,
the police, the army, the protectors of the rich and powerful in control,
were turned by family members to become morally whole,
to turn back to the 'Human way',
to Save Earth Every Day,
a return of 'Soft Care' kept them there.
This was their need and this was their Seed.
Saving Earth Every Day

The girl slowed down and went into quiet time, as she had been taught when she wanted to focus, while sensing herself and remembering her classes of the day she realized the solution for travelling around the mountains unimpeded.

She had seen in the old 'hollow-bilds' of history 'Gliding Boards' with wheels, for standing on, they looked like fun, she must talk to some of the students who worked with the energy technology about that, she thought of a more practical design, lightweight, solar energised and self-renewing. Just like the suit.

She was happy for that thought; the design would allow safe and on-going maintenance of our planet. In a world of limited resources these things were needed, especially for the coming Heat.

She remembered one of the poems of the '99'

The Hero lies within us all
you must only listen to its call,
it speaks to you in a silent way,
and it does so every day.

When you're quiet and you can sense,
you begin to feel the Hero's presence.
Sometimes you'll turn your back and look away,
that's okay, one day – you won't.
It makes no difference who you are, you can all strive to be a Hero,
it's just above you, it's not far, jump and you will catch that rope,
for you are that Hero, you are that hope.

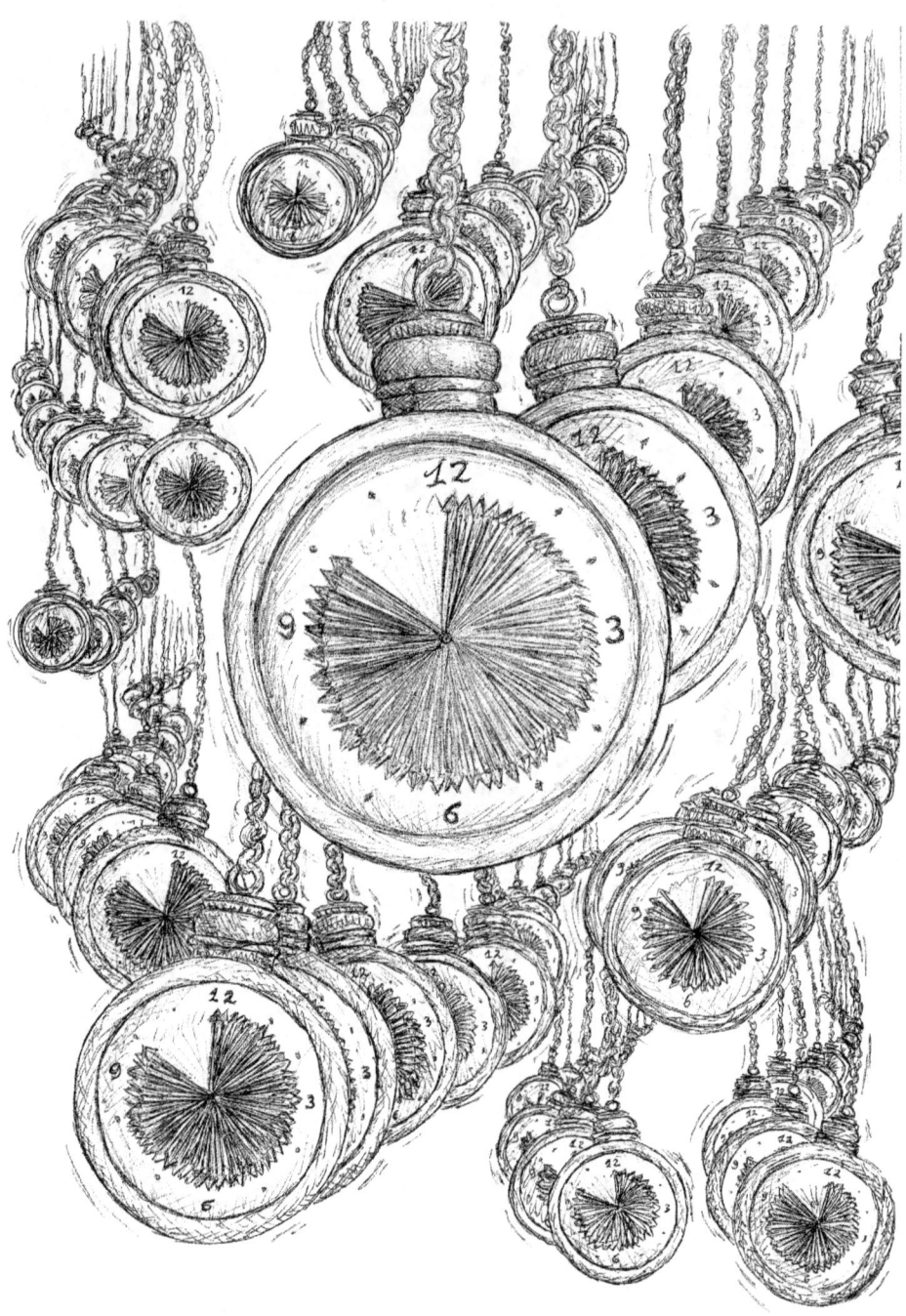

A long time before – now – Present Time

Rise of the Heroes

She read the first words of the website again.

> The Heroes that saved the world from Hell,
> the Heroes rose because they had a story to tell,
> tales of ancient, tales of old.
> We must become Heroes, we must become bold.
> It's something that the rich never thought would sell.
> Join a movement, do it now, boycott the companies from Hell.

It was time, it was now, if it was going to ever happen it had to be now. Everybody knew it; it was on everybody's lips, unfortunately governments everywhere were observing everything, the 'leeks' had shown what everybody knew, but not enough cared about that - yet, that would change.

It was disaster after disaster in one way or another; wars of control in the poorer countries and wars of austerity in the richer ones. With the climate changes affecting so many places on the planet, it was amazing that there were still deniers.

She had read somewhere that a study showed that these people only watched programs or read news that backed up their thinking, well, that's like only looking in the magic mirror that keeps you thinking you're pretty, or 'I'm alright Jack'. Well the mirrors cracked honey, get a reality hit and keep apace, we're humans in a race.

So many people were now joining one movement or another; they were right, the way we all lived was wrong, everybody knew that, but that wasn't just the point, it was the time of action. A generation left to slow down Climate Change, after that, the door was shut. The planet's hitched a ride on a speeding train and the only light at the end of the tunnel seems to be the warming sun.

All these actions were in progress, all over the world. Many of her friends no longer did or talked about the same things anymore, they talked about their actions and not so much of trivia, it was as if a competition had started and in reality many had.

There were so many actions happening, the internet was full of videos, of people doing stuff, those were the ones that had the most 'Hits' all the time now, it was the biggest thing ever. No-one knew how big this was going to be, but everybody said society would have to change, everybody had something to say.

The 'occupy camps' were everywhere, occupying everything they could, that was dangerous sometimes, as the police no longer protected the people, only the powerful in control. That would start to change when their kids speak to them, she thought. 'Hi dad, what do you do about Global Warming?' 'Oh, I protect the people that are causing it son'. 'Why?'

Hell, even all the dance competitions were dancing for social change, not just for the climate but for social justice, people were connecting it all up together. Suddenly it was the only thing to do, to have a 'social responsibility'. If a boy wanted to impress you these days, he would tell you what he was doing. Soon enough actions were all over the internet. There's no way to escape this new social responsibility now, everybody knew about the wars of resources, and the predicted coming ones over water supplies.

She looked at another website

Silence through Fear

Silence through fear is a common thing, we all suffer from its sting,
it should be forgiven and not held to account,
we are all silent, this we find out.

It's said these days we have a 'culture of conceit',
well yes, but who is the driver in the seat,
the culture of ideas was meant to lead humanity to a question,
could each individual have a clearer perception,
about themselves in their role in the world they live,
is there something more they had to give, or become?

We've allowed our society to come to a place, a state, where our children
and we will have an increasingly warmer fate,
this will become clear with passing time,
but it's the 'silence of the good people' that kills something so fine.

The wall of silence, invisible to the eye, but it's a strong wall, little gets by,
it's a wall that's fed and built with bricks of fear,
it's a wall where there is no humanity near.
Humanity's guilt must be forgiven,
for it's hard to look at oneself and say, 'there is something wrong,
this is not where we belong'.
This is something we hold dear, but we are silent through fear.

She too was frightened and felt helpless but didn't want to be silent, not
while the world around her was 'Heating', and there were so many voices
trying to be heard in the dark. She hit a new site.

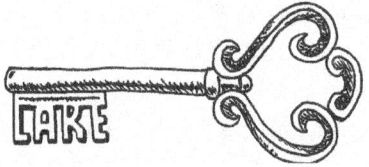

Keys, Locks and Chains

What is the right Key for change? What's possible, what lies in our range?
What do you think? What do you feel?
Do you believe you are young and should have some fun?
Or do you think there is more meaning to your life?
Can you the 'Hero' become
because the older generations did succumb?

Instead 'they' put the idea in comics and films and manipulated us, the
young, all for profit and all for the same song to be sung.

Carrots on a string: T.V. shows that will make you famous if you can dance,
sing or anything really, break a world record, set a new pace in our modern
society called humans in a consumer race.

They give you 'Heroes' for your age,
everybody needs it, it's always the rage,

someone you will try to be like, it's a drink that they spike,
it keeps you subdued and under control.
On T.V. or in films, what film star said a speech,
that kept you in their reach,
to make you feel it's just for you,
oh yes, you could have said that too.

There's a fire outside and it's burning at the door.
'Oh I heard it all before, yup, 'fire at the door',
of course it's there to an extent,
but we're ok, honey, make sure you pay the rent.'

This is depressing, moving on, she hit the button again. She liked lots of film stars, it's not their fault, that's the work they do and they often inspire people in good things. Many work for changes in the world.

She liked some of the songs that were now out, but a lot of them were violent in their intentions, or negative in their outlook, calling for revolution. In some ways she agreed, but from what she read it should be a movement in revolution of thought. But of course if the 'Let them eat cake' mentality of the rich did not change and keep up with the times, well, let's hope they all speak French.

She hit a new rap song

Complacency and Comply

New methods of surveillance and control, humans improve in the hypnotic indoctrination show. It's generally accepted that this is how it is and will go.
No dissent, no repeal,
T.V. street lightning will be real.
You are tracked as you take a walk, never free to talk,
except about the trivia supplied to you
to keep you occupied with nothing better to do.
With long term plans in the making
your life's been organized for the taking.

'The young of the world, born and bred, many left unfed,
but as to our own kids, in their minds we've sown the seeds of complacency
and comply, join the consumer currency,
don't question why.
We'll occupy you with the process of fear,
you will soon come to live and adapt, for we'll embed it in every app.

If you're poor and live in a country that has something that we need,
well, for a while we'll bomb and kill you till you bleed,
then eventually, you'll want to try
everything that we sell that you can buy, it will just take a generation or two
till the older ones die - out,
cause we'll breed it in you. What life's about?
You will serve us very well, till the planet burns like Hell.'

So you're young, still having fun, it's what the young should do.
To live this life on its new tracks every day,
but to Global Warming - you have a say,
unfortunately not long young people, 15 years max,
then the speeding train is off the tracks.
To the future you are the Key – if you want to be.

As much as she agreed with the words, it was enough to do your brain in. A bit on the extremely depressing side, it kinda makes you prefer the option of digging your own grave with a teaspoon rather than trying to do anything against Global Warming. What about Life is Magical and Miraculous and we have something to live for. I know all that negative stuff, I'm aware of all that.

She read a site that denied Global Warming. What were these people thinking; everyone knew that scientists that spoke in denial of Global Warming received their funding through some form of 'think tank' organizations, why did they bother anymore. They'd only get clicks from the 'same set mentality' brigade.

Although, she quietly pondered on why and answered herself: to keep us occupied with anything that would divert our attention, energy and time away from doing something worthwhile. With so many people occupied with world sport competitions or beauty contests, reality T.V. shows. What a reality, few of these people on T.V. ever discussed how the world will be soon. They've been side-tracked by the media machine and their search for 15 minutes of fame.

She pinned a piece of paper to the wall, she had been sketching as she always did, casually, it helped her remember. It was like a mind map for her, she loved the way Leonardo used to mind-map his work, bits and pieces of everything on the same page and mirror writing to keep things secret. He was encrypting his work way back then, she thought. But she wondered if Leonardo had realised where some of his ideas of weapons led, and what he would think of that today. She hit another page.

Truth I cannot face

Let's presume our purpose was not to live the life we have,
but to live the life that's waiting to be lived,
the path that lies unseen, if we didn't see it then it's never been – yet.

Sit down, have a beer, switch on the telly, 'oh look at that dear,
another new blockbuster film to see.
It's about the world that was and the world to be
because right now it's changing rapidly'.
What better cause could humans find,
to return from the land of the living blind?
Have fun when you watch T.V.
Is this really all you wanted to be?

Yes, she thought, 'The life that's waiting to be lived'; there's a path that were not taking yet. She came back to herself. Why wasn't she doing anything?

She hit the button again.

Powers in control set the stage for the play
through their actions, but not only, things will not fare well,
for 'Being-less' leaders will have no understanding to tell,
how all will or should be.
They read their script and speak as a puppet on a string,
'Being-less' leaders always seem to speak as if they know everything,
perfect actions in a play, lost in their role day after day,
so deeply taken they are mistaken
about what they were meant to be.

True, she thought, but now politicians in every country if they wanted votes couldn't afford not to speak up, they were now frightened but speaking empty words as always, this was not enough anymore, no-one was prepared to put up with emptiness. Not as we destroyed our only home and it would burn. Most just didn't feel the effects yet, at least not in the rich countries. The future is beside us now, buy buckets of suntan lotion she thought. I suppose if you're smart you'd take out shares in the company that makes it.

She had read the words 'Drill Baby Drill', and that they were searching everywhere for more places to drill for fossil fuels. What a thought, what a mentality, don't these people care about their kids. We've already been told that we can't burn up all the known reserves on the planet and yet they spend enough money each year that would feed the world over, *just searching for more*, under the melting ice, under the oceans, what is it these so called 'Leaders' aren't seeing? What is it they lack in their 'being'?

She was starting to wonder if she was dropped off on the wrong planet. She hit another site.

The good and bad sides of Global Warming

These points are considered at different time frames, the near and the not so far away.

On the good side - you won't need much winter clothing.

On the bad side - there won't be any clothing to get, due to social unrest and interruption of normal capitalist businesses.

On the good side - you won't need to water the flowers.

On the bad side - there won't be any.

On the good side - it will be warm.

On the bad side - it will be too warm for life as we know it.

On the good side - in some places you'll get more rain.

On the bad side - the rain will come with hurricanes like we have never experienced before.

On the good side - you know not to invest near the coast.

On the bad side - if you have already, difficult to sell.

On the good side - no need to worry about visiting the north and south poles of our planet.

On the bad side - they won't be there.

On the good side - no need to worry about sharks.

On the bad side - the water will be too acidic to go in.

On the good side – the ocean will be closer to your door.

On the bad side - In many places it will be over your house.

On the good side - people will be less concerned with inane trivia.

On the bad side - by then, there will be no inane trivia, only survival.

On the good side - many people will travel.

On the bad side - they will be fleeing the devastating effects of a warming planet, in search of water or food.

On the good side - there will be airborne computerized drones for controlling traffic across and within countries.

On the bad side - they will be weaponized.

On the good side - people will feel more together in their desperation.

On the bad side - public dissent will be violently repressed.

On the good side - survival courses will become the norm.

On the bad side - it won't be choice, but necessity.

On the good side - you will have empathy with what the dinosaurs went through.

On the bad side - look at what happened to them.

That's enough of that she thought. Fun, but If I want I can make my own list of depression and repression.

Boycotts were everywhere; competitions were made to see how quickly how many people joined the latest boycott. They were on every social media. There were lists that people kept adding their names too.

Sure, some big financial organizations divest from fossil fuels, 'it's up for consideration', 'slowly over time'. What are they thinking, there is no time. It's countdown to catastrophe time and they won't even put the stopwatch on?

Some other companies were losing so much money they were posting their apologies all over the place, saying they were committed to going green, no one believed them anymore. Everybody knew they lied as policy. It was just rebranding. She made a song to remind her of this, as well as drawing that's how she mapped and remembered the information. Her mum used to sing her a list of the things she had to remember to do in the day. It always worked.

Lie and deny until you're caught,
then contain the damage you brought,
you can do it every day, just say it in a different way.
The public really want to believe you so;
therefore you can lead them a 'round the 'merry go'.

Some companies tried to commercialize these movements, they too were boycotted and the bigger companies in charge of them. Everybody knew who owned what now. Those lists were sent all over the place. Lots of things were encrypted these days, encryption instructions were being sent to everyone. Ah, she thought, everybody copies all Leonardo's work some time. The heat was hot. And not just for our planet. She read something else.

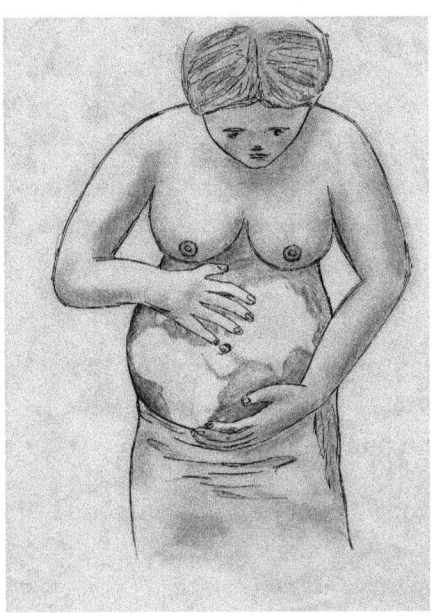

Compassion

How can a Hero awaken on such a scale
that would make all other movements by comparison pale?
To awaken to the need to realize all humans bleed,
that all you see and those to come
will have a warming fate and they will burn.

The pull of barbarism is a powerful force,
for in the end that's where this pull leads of course.
Humans slid back down to the savage state;
the house was shut with a lock on the gate.
No way to return, we let our home planet burn.

Probably, only the power of compassion on a massive scale,
could tame the dragon that does prevail.
The permanent realization of certain extinction,
that all our children will die 'the warming death'.

It seems we need to be taught how to cultivate compassion;
it might be the antidote to the patient being ill.
We of course, are the patient,
for at a certain temperature everything ceases to be, there is no pill.

The message that came through was clear, it had to be collective; but for that to happen, people had to wake up first to the terror and immediacy of the problem. For that, they had to be affected; it had to be personal as well, for no one got involved if they didn't connect into the coming disaster.

Lots of people knew they should do something but were lost as to what they could do. A generation left of chance. It had to begin now, now as in yesterday already.

The new generation of young songsters had every right to be angry, you get angry when you feel sorrow and don't have any power to do anything about what you feel is unjust.

No wonder they were singing about the seeds of change. She played another.

SEED

There are no politicians in our range,
who have the personal power to bring change,
they are weak and they are bought,
and they are not what we sought.
We seek a change, it must be social;
it must be for the common good.
And if all the young could join this cause,
then succeed we would.

There is a movement and it's called SEED
and it will grow with our need,
it stands for Saving Earth Every Day,
there is something you can do, in your own way.

All it needs is for you to become aware,
not just of you, but of everything that is out there.

'They' condition us when we are young,
and 'they' only have one song they want to be sung.
'Join our happy merry little way, buy new things every day,
we'll take your money and your time,
and you'll be so 'Occupied', you'll think you're fine.

We'll give you fashion and great things to buy, lots of new stuff to try,
we'll give you a voice and give you a vote,
but we'll stifle it in your throat.
There's no way we'll let you speak,
we'll give you drugs to make you weak
and even them you'll have to buy
if you want to continue to live the lie.

You will think that all is fine, but we really control your mind.
Take all the actions that you like, whatever you drink, we will spike.
We have the greatest media minds in the world in our pay.
Hell, we give them more money every day.
They will place our stuff in your mind, and we even tell you,
because we know you're blind.'

Well now our eyes are open and our mouths are too,
and we know just what to do.
Become a Hero, take the path,
don't deviate - incur their wrath.
The cause is greater than we know,
our planet's melting down below.

Well yes, that kind of makes the point doesn't it? The girl was watching the screen intently, more and more videos of actions were going up every day. Maybe she should start one, but what? She had already joined lots of boycotts, all worthwhile and connected together; she went on marches, which was more exciting and meaningful than sitting watching the black box. 'The fascinating world of hypnotizing banality.'

Switch on – switch off – sit and stare –
don't think about anything happening out there.

Smiling at herself, she realized the contradiction within as she looked at a smaller 'black magic box' and was being inspired.

What else could she do? From what she understood so far about all this, it was not to make people feel bad about themselves, people don't need to be made to feel guilty that they drive cars or fly all over the world, although she did like that newspaper writer saying something like 'when you fly, other people die, it's as simple as that'. Of course there's a point there, but nothing compared to the war machine and the other largest consumers of oil in the world.

If enough organizations divert their interests away from oil, then at some point oil would rise in price, then you're dealing with the transportation, plane and auto industries, which then would have to be restructured, as well as new ways of building cities.

She thought to herself this is 'Mission Impossible', Aka Global Change, 'no way Jose', but what else is there to do. This is apocalyptic, it's not about little weather fluctuations.

Sure, companies have their profits to make, but if there's millions on the move and millions dying, coastal cities disappearing, no grain productions, no clean water to drink for the many. Then the only people that will be making any money will be the pharmaceutical companies, supplying the cures for the new airborne diseases that will occur and that don't need oil to fly around the world. That and the Matrix of companies involved in WAR.

If only Sean Connery were king of the world, he'd fix it, she thought. Everybody loved Sean, why didn't he do that before he got too old.

She went to her favourite page, the one that was for kids of all ages.

Poems of Lala

Lala is a puppet with lots of stories to tell,
but she decided to branch out a little
to help out the people on a planet that wasn't very well.

Seeds of Hope

Guess what, do we have a story for you,
the planet's heating up, what can we do?

I bet that there are lots of things that you can say,
and I bet that you can think of something new every day.
Some may work out just fine, and some may take a little bit of time.

But really it's just planting a seed, and waiting for it to grow;
you don't see what happens underneath the ground down below.
Seeds begin to grow in the dark,
something happens to light that spark.

It's a spark of life when something takes root, the roots go down and spread
outwards in space, it's just as if they're in a race,
that gives it power to stay connected,
and it's all in the dark, it's undetected,
but at the same time, something reaches upwards to gain a higher ground
and to humans all this happens without a sound,
a little water, a little care,
and suddenly you have a plant growing there.

Now that seed may become a flower or a tree,
or it may be the seed of an idea that comes from you or me.
Ideas come, some stay, some take root and grow,
many pass on bye and some we don't want to know,
but some ideas will grow in you, just like that seed,
and it may become so passionate it becomes a need.

To save our planet many ideas will come from you
or other people you know, some will know just what to do.

Time counts, it's running out, we need to sing, dance and shout,
and a Global Warming is what it's all about.
We need to turn the heat back down;
it's just not as simple as it sounds.
There are a few problems in our way,
big companies and politicians block what we say.
We need a movement for one and all.

Global Warming must be something to talk about every day,
to help people have a voice,
because everybody's got something to say,
and everybody has a choice.

Me - I - You

I was there when you were young;
I am the song that should be sung.
I am that voice deep in you
that tells you something that you always knew.
It's in every fairy story or legend you've been told,
it tells you that now you should be bold,
to rise, to wake, to actions take.

You went into a life and fell asleep,
and your inner voice it did keep.
Life silenced what you knew; it gave you toys to occupy you,
now these you're taught to want to need to buy,
it´s just a lie.

You joined something called the consumer plot,
things they sold, but in real it was you that was bought, that's sad,
you know that too, you can feel it when you listen to you.

But now 'All Life' needs you to awake,
it's your planet that's now at stake.
Listen to that voice again, there are no words, it's your best friend,
it lets you know something's wrong,
it never makes a dance or song.

It's quiet, it makes you feel, but only for a moment, what isn't real,
then it goes silent, and it will stay away
until you do something in your day
that shows that you it did hear, and that you value that it's near.
For it's the closest thing to you,
sometimes you're quiet and this you knew.

The Heroes

That conscience is there it's just buried deep,
so much piled on top it went to sleep.
It needs a prince to come and kiss to awaken once again,
or a Hero to be your friend.
There's a Hero in us all, you just need to listen to your inner call.
It's in your emotions, it's what you feel.
It's the only Hero that is really real.

You have that Hero in you, it was taught to you when you were young,
this you knew.
You just went to sleep with so much of life to do.
To live, gain experiences, get older and thrive,
but now it needs the Hero in us all if our planet's to survive.

And those Heroes have much work to do,
some will protest, this is true,
others will with others speak, perhaps it's you,

Some may be a Hero with their songs,
it's a common voice, it has to be, there is no choice.
But you can be the Hero in many a way and you can do it every day.
A Hero with compassion always has something to say.

Perhaps there is no Hero, no Prince nor Princess
in these people anymore,
in whom the Goddess of greed and uncaring does possess,
'all for me and none for you',
it's their motto and dragon that the Hero must slay too.
Perhaps in some it could be awakened, that I do not know.
But that Hero is you, are you listening? What will you do?

The girl was quiet and pondering all the information she had read the whole evening. Where did her talents lie? What was she good at? Or what could she learn about, to learn something new, things she had never even considered before, but she wanted to combine what she felt strongly about with what she was good at. She was quiet and aware for a while.

As far as she could see at the moment she had two options; the first was to activate more kids in her school into joining an action. A school project where the kids themselves would be the contributors, producing books of art, poetry, songs, drawings and paintings. It's all possible these days with the internet. She knew this was happening in places, but not in her school yet.

She typed out the first of her thoughts for the project.

In order to comprehend the magnitude of our problem kids would have to become directly informed, search, compile and discuss the information. It's a communal education of sharing the efforts, but it's also personal self-motivated involvement.

It's so important to inspire and involve the generation of kids that are still in school, in ways that are not only intellectual, factual, and often dry or even boring and especially not just doom and gloom. But instead collectively stimulating, causing them to have their own involvement, discussion, debate, education and various expressions.

This would educate the generation of kids that will be directly affected by Global Warming, bringing it to the forefront of their awareness, causing them to be affected, and inspired to be pro-active in saving their only planet home.

This will be the generation that will leave school soon and will try to find employment, even perhaps in positions of power; there is a limited time frame of opportunity for possible positive action. And it's the young that are the hope and that can bring change – if they are self-inspired – the elders will be dead and will not face the consequences of their own inactions regarding Global Warming.

This generation are the new artists, these projects could help to guide and inspire their intellectual and emotional involvement for the rest of their life, there is no way of knowing what that underground river could feed.

Shock of shocks, poetry becomes re-energised for modern consumption, of course it may be more rap orientated; after all, things change, Shakespeare was modern in his time. Who knows where the next Shakespeare, Blake, Thoreau or Maya Angelou lives, or where the next da Vinci is, she or he might be sitting in your classroom every day, waiting to be awoken, they are there, waiting to be inspired, just waiting for that spark to light the flame that would burn eternal.

We have an underground reservoir of untapped potential that just needs to be let loose and pointed towards an aim, a target; we are the bow and in this case we are also the arrow and we really do have a target. Our aim is towards this collective need. It redirects this generation towards the most important theme in our history, humanity's survival.

Without kids being involved there may be no hope, and there will be no change, we are being bought up and redirected, re-managed and rebranded by the rich and powerful. But kids need a cause, they need a spark to light a flame, for this truly is a case of 'to be or not to be', it signifies whether 'I am or I am not'. They need to be the hero for each other.

Imagine what that art would inspire, all kids involved in all aspects of writing, painting and producing in print, on line, or performing on stage their works and their art books of poetry or stories of Global Warming Awareness. The kids themselves could go to other schools to explain the benefits, financially, educationally, personally and globally. Imagine those leaving school in a year or two and what they would do, painting, filming, art, directing, entering politics, saving our world in many small and great ways. All influenced by their collective work in producing a work of Awareness Art in school.

These projects would make money from all the families and friends, grandparents, aunts and uncles of the kids involved, local but it could also be Global, that would help the school itself or to finance other projects.

Those older teenagers with more advanced computer skills could set it all up in design and graphics for a book etc. They can easily care for all those aspects while developing their skills there. Teachers have the ability already to edit, some of them are language experts, co-join to another school in another country, double language more publicity, excellent.

What fun, humour, sadness, would rise from the depths, what rage and sorrow for our world tomorrow, which is now today. What Heroes would wake and rise to that call from within.

That was it; she would revise and go for that later.

Her second option was more personal and immediate.

She was good at drawing; she wanted to work with Art and Design when she left school. She'd start a site for web-works for Global Warming, she had seen a few already, some free and some commercialized. She'd offer click buttons to see who got the most ratings, she had a friend who could organize that, she was sure he'd love to join into that. She just had to do the drawings and paintings.

She cancelled her plans that evening and started working on her new project; she began the first draft and sketches. The first words were...

ART Works for Global Warming

SEEDS

Of

SOFT CARE

Saving Earth Every Day Somewhere

Saving Our Future Today – Can Always Remember Earth

Here - now - today - I open this site
for 'Pictures and Poems' to help bring justice in our dark night,
and the night is dark my friends but it's getting warm,
as I get older I'll want my children to belong
to a world that's 'Just' and not spinning out of control,
with the politicians pushing us down the 'Memory Hole'.
For pictures or poems that get hits, there will be a prize,
you get to look your child in the eyes –
and say, I did that.

People of the world, this is a seed;
it needs to grow, water it, start the show.
Create some art to give your view;
you know there's something you can do.
This movement has now begun;
join it, so you can Draw-Baby-Draw,
instead of Burn-Baby-Burn.
I'll give you a badge you can wear
or make your own if you dare,
the point is simple,
about your planet and our future to care.

First Poem and Picture

SOFT - CARE

Saving Our Future Today – Can Always Remember Earth

It's always nice to keep it short, all those things that are usually bought. The world of acronyms is always there, especially today, but here's the title of this page, soft care – it should be all the rage.

Saving Our Future Today – Can Always Remember Earth

CARE: of course is always good,
it's what humans would do if they could,
if they were left to work it out
and were not controlled from the media shout.
And Earth needs a remembering, it's where we tread every day;
we all know this in some way.
Of all the things we can do and we can spend our time,
a little bit of care for Earth would be softly fine.

Something needed as we run out of time.

Kept by controllers in the dark, 'occupied' to play in the park,
full of amusements and things to buy as our planet starts to fry.

SOFT: Saving Our Future Today: relevant due to the urgency of the
situation, from Global Warming there's no cessation,
but there is a window of opportunity,
it's just the future's misty, never clear enough to see,
but it's there it can be had,
it needs a struggle and not to stay in silence and be sad.

A soft revolution in thought,
why? Because it's the attitude of the old and rich that must no longer be
bought. Revolutions are always repressed in well managed ways,
putting people to the test, many die with much suffering – societies and
cultures destroyed, if those in power they have annoyed.

Organized wars for 100 years, mostly politics played on fears.

So a SOFT revolution of thought spread through the world today,
it needs the young to have a say.
Those in lands that are oppressed have no voice,
survival is their only quest, to make it through and survive another day -
understandable - it needs the young of the western world,
who still have a voice and still have a say.

Of course it's weak, there is no movement,
in the last ten years there's no real improvement.
Some things are happening here and there,
about divestment from oil stocks, people now care,
it activates the young and old and people to be bold.

It needs a revolution of thought and care for peaceful actions everywhere,
there's so many things you can do, it needs to affect the old, the rich too,
sure maybe they'll just care for profit and shares, well, that's what they do,
it's in the system like superglue.

A SOFT revolution of care, affecting everyone, to raise their voice for one
cause, Real Global Warming Laws,
would affect a change in all societies.

Wars could never be allowed – isn't that a dream that we would love to be
seen. Politicians would be cowed into submission for the greater good.
Ah, if only they could.

15 years max and you're off the tracks,
so you wanna play around or get off your backs,
stand up to raise your voice,
make a soft care revolution your choice.

If you get violent you'll be repressed,
and the rich have media, you know it's the best.
Everything can be well managed,
except saving a planet that we have damaged.

Then attention will be taken and people will be shaken – down again by
well-chosen media information, you know the situation,
you live it every day, the old, the rich of now will all be dead,
by the time real heat hits your head.

So it's 15 years max, just to keep the train on the tracks.

You never know what you can do, even you,
there are so many real people in this world of Being-less leaders,
you are the leaders, you are the young,
it's your song that needs to be sung.
Don't be conned anymore by 'Being-less' leaders who don't lead,
you need a planet and you have a planet in need.

At no time in the history of the human mystery has it been more important
for people to come together, to have a collective voice
and at no point has it been more difficult due to bad laws and governing and
multiple surveillance of choice,
and at no point in time will we ever have this slight window of possibility
again, one voice one cause, it needs millions of you.
To be true and to ask yourself, what you can do.

Here are the pictures and words I give, hit it, so it can live,
then do your own and start a craze, for we will live in warmer days.
We are the young and we must the Heroes of old become.
They are ancient, they had their day,
we are here now and we have a say.

We have a cause, new world laws,
we have a choice,
we don't have to be silent, we have a voice.
And we must raise it, whether in rage or sorrow,
for now today is tomorrow.
You can Save Earth Every Day Somewhere,
we have a need you are the seed.
Become a Hero.